Yes, No, Maybe: A Teen's Guide to Pendulums

Copyright © 2025 by Dr. Constance Santego.

Copy Editor & Interior Design: Constance Santego
Book Layout: ©2017 BookDesignTemplates.com

Ordering Information:
Quantity sales. Special discounts are available on quantity purchases by corporations, associations, and others. For details, contact the "Special Sales Department" at the address above.

Trade Paperback ISBN: 978-1-990062-89-6
eBook ISBN 978-1-990062-90-2
Created and published In Canada. Printed and bound in the United States of America

First Edition
Published by Maximillian Enterprises
Kelowna, BC
Canada
www.constancesantego.ca

Yes, No, Maybe:
A Teen's Guide To Pendulums

When Google or Chat Can't Answer Your Questions

Dr. Constance Santego

Maximillian Enterprises
Kelowna, BC

Dedication

To the seekers, the skeptics, and the secretly curious—
this book is for you.

For every teen who dares to ask bold questions,
and every adult who remembers what it feels like to wonder.

May your pendulum always guide you,
not just to answers,
but back to the wisdom you carry inside yourself.

— Dr. Constance Santego

"If you want to find the secrets of the universe, think in terms of energy, frequency and vibration."
— *Nikola Tesla*

ALSO BY DR. CONSTANCE SANTEGO

NOVELS

Illegitimate Grace
Ashcroft Hollow

Okanagan Trilogy:
Beneath the Vineyards
Under the Okanagan Sun
Guardian of the Lake

The Nine Spiritual Gifts Series:
Journey of a Soul – (Vol 1 Michael)
Language of a Soul – (Vol 2 Gabriel)
Prophecy of a Soul – (Vol 3 Bath Kol)
Healing of a Soul – (Vol 4 Raphael)
Miracles of a Soul – (Vol 5 Hamied)
Knowledge of a Soul – (Vol 6 Raziel)
Wisdom of a Soul – (Vol 7 Uriel)
Faith of a Soul – (Vol 8 Pistis Sophia)

NONFICTION
The Intuitive Life, The Gift Of Prophecy, Third Edition
Fairy Tales, Dreams And Reality... Where Are You On Your Path?
Second Edition
Your Persona... The Mask You Wear
Archangel Michael's Soul Retrieval Guide
Tesla And The Future Of Energy Medicine
Beyond Tesla: Advancing The Science Of Energy Healing
Tesla's Code: Mastering Energy, Frequency, And Creative Power
Beyond The Mind: Harnessing The Power Of Astral Projection For
Creative Awakening
Bend, Don't Break: Finding Your Way Back To Abundance
Ring Therapy: A Guide To Healing And Balance
Ring Therapy Pocket Guide
Floraopathy™: The Art And Science Of Vibrational Healing With
Essential Oils
Dear Older Me: A Memoir... Of Sorts
It's Just Like Poker: A Spiritual Guide To Playing The
Cards Life Deals You
Signs And Meanings: What The Feet Reveal About Health, Stress,
And The Body's Story
Auricions: Unlocking Subconscious Healing Through Quantum
Medicine
Quick Fix Acupressure Method

Type 3 Diabetes: *The Hidden Link Between Blood Sugar, Brain Health, and Healing Naturally*
Manifestation – The DREAM Method in 5 Steps

REIKI WISDOM, SERIES:
Angelic Lifestyle, a Vibrant Lifestyle
Angelic Lifestyle 42-Day Energy Cleanse
Reiki and the Power of The Joint Points: Unlocking Energy Pathways for Healing (Vol I)
Reiki and Karmic Healing: Releasing Patterns From Past Lives (Vol II)
Reiki and the Five Elements (Vol III)
Secrets of a Healer, Magic Of Reiki
The Reiki Master's Manual

SECRETS OF A HEALER, SERIES:
Magic Of Aromatherapy (Vol I)
Magic Of Reflexology (Vol II)
Magic Of The Gifts (Vol III)
Magic Of Muscle Testing (Vol IV)
Magic Of Iridology (Vol V)
Magic Of Massage (Vol VI)
Magic Of Hypnotherapy (Vol VII)
Magic Of Reiki (Vol VIII)
Magic Of Advanced Aromatherapy (Vol IX)
Magic Of Esthetics (Vol X)
The Reiki Master's Manual (Vol XI)

ADULT COLORING JOURNALS
SERIES-ZEN COLORING:
Quantum Energy and Mindful Living Journal (Vol 1)
Reiki Energy Journal (Vol 2)
Nine Spiritual Gifts Journal (Vol 3)
I Forgive Journal (Vol 4)

FOR CHILDREN
I am Big Tonight. I Don't Need the Light

COOKBOOK
My Favorite Recipes, with a Hint of Giggle

BUISNESS

HUMOR/GIFT BOOK

Contents

Preface

When you first hear the word *pendulum*, you might picture a clock swinging back and forth, or maybe a hypnotist's pocket watch dangling before someone's eyes. But a pendulum can be much more than that. It can be a bridge between your conscious mind and the quiet whispers of your intuition.

This book was born out of curiosity. I wanted to know: *Why does a simple weight on a string seem to answer questions? Is it science? Is it magic? Or is it something in between?* Along the way, I discovered the truth: it's all of the above. The pendulum works through the subtle, unconscious signals your body emits, while simultaneously opening a door to a deeper, more playful relationship with your inner knowing.

I wrote this book for teenagers—because teens are often brave enough to try something new without overthinking it. But I also wrote it for adults, because sometimes we forget how to play, experiment, and wonder. A pendulum is for anyone willing to stay curious.

Inside, you'll find a mix of history, science, fun experiments, and creative tools. You'll learn how to make your own pendulum, train it to give yes/no answers, and expand its use with charts, games, and energy practices. Most importantly, you'll learn how to use it as a set of training wheels for your intuition—until you no longer need it.

This isn't a book of rigid rules. It's an invitation. Every experiment, every chart, every swing of the pendulum is a chance to discover something about yourself.

So as you read, let yourself play. Ask silly questions. Ask serious ones. Try the experiments, laugh when it surprises you, and write down what you discover.

Because the real magic of the pendulum isn't in the string or the weight—it's in you.

Note to Reader

Before we dive in, I want you to know one thing: this book is not about giving you all the answers. It's about showing you how to ask better questions.

A pendulum is not a magic fortune-teller, and it's not a replacement for your own judgment or professional advice. What it *is*—is a tool. A mirror. A way to connect with the signals your body and mind are already sending you.

Think of this book like a guide to experimenting. Some of the exercises will feel light and fun. Others may feel surprisingly deep. You don't have to do them all at once, and you don't have to take anything as absolute truth. Try what resonates, skip what doesn't, and keep an open mind.

Most of all, remember this: you are always in charge. The pendulum isn't here to control you—it's here to support you. Your intuition is the real compass. The pendulum just makes it easier to notice the direction it's pointing.

So read with curiosity. Play with the experiments. And let this be a safe space to explore your own inner wisdom.

Disclaimer: This book is intended for personal exploration, learning, and entertainment purposes. It is not a substitute for professional medical, legal, or financial advice. Always seek qualified guidance for serious decisions or health concerns.

— Dr. Constance Santego

How to Use This Book

This isn't a boring school textbook. It's more like a game guide for your intuition. You don't have to read every page in order—just jump in where it looks fun.

🔍 1. Be Curious

You don't need special skills. Just an open mind (and something dangly).

🎲 2. Play the Experiments

Each chapter has a little "Try This" challenge. Don't just read—actually try them. That's when the pendulum gets cool.

🎨 3. Make It Yours

The charts and wheels here are just starters. Doodle on them, make new ones, or ask the silliest questions you can think of.

😆 4. Mix Silly + Serious

"Should I eat this pizza?" and "What's my vibe today?" are both fair game. Have fun with both.

📖 5. Keep a Log

Jot down what your pendulum says. Later, you'll be like: "Whoa, it was right!" (or "Wow, that was random," which is just as useful).

🔋 6. Keep It Chill

Pendulums = self-exploration. Not medical advice. Not crystal-ball fortune-telling. Keep it safe and empowering.

Pro Tip: There's no wrong way to use this book. If you're curious enough to pick up a pendulum, you're already doing it right.

Yes, No, Maybe: A Teen's Guide To Pendulums

When Google or Chat Can't Answer Your Questions

Dr. Constance Santego

Introduction: Yes, No, Maybe

Why This Book Is Written for Teens (and Why Adults Secretly Need It, Too)

Let's be real: teenagers are way braver than most adults when it comes to trying new, weird, and slightly mysterious things. While grown-ups are busy worrying about whether something is "scientifically proven" or "socially acceptable," teens just *do it.*

That's why this book is written for you. You don't need years of meditation practice, a degree in physics, or some expensive spiritual toolkit. You just need a curious mind, a little object on a string, and a willingness to experiment.

But—confession—this book is also for adults.
Because here's the secret: adults are basically teenagers with more bills. They still want clarity. They still wonder if they're on the right path. They still wish for a quick way to get answers when they're stuck. The difference? Adults sometimes forget how to have fun while learning.

So, if you're a teen, welcome, this is your playground.
And if you're an adult: don't worry, you're totally allowed in. In fact, you might find your inner teenager waking up while you read—and that's a very good thing.

WHAT IS THIS BOOK ABOUT?

At its simplest, it's about a pendulum: a weight on a string that swings when you ask it questions. Sounds silly, right? But here's the kicker: when it moves, it's not random. It's responding to *you.*

Scientists call it the **ideomotor effect**—tiny, invisible muscle movements triggered by your subconscious mind. Healers call it **energy in motion**—your intuition speaking through your body. You can call it whatever you like, but here's the truth: it works.

This book will teach you how to use a pendulum to:

- Ask clear yes/no/maybe questions.
- Check in with your body and emotions.
- Play games that actually strengthen your intuition.
- Explore energy fields (yours, your pet's, even your snacks).
- Decide between two (or more) choices when you're torn.

WHY "YES, NO, MAYBE"?

Because that's the first language of the pendulum, you'll start by training your pendulum to show you "yes," "no," and "maybe." But pretty soon, you'll realize it's really about something deeper: learning how to say yes to yourself, no to what drains you, and maybe to possibilities you haven't discovered yet.

YOUR FIRST MINI EXPERIMENT

I don't want you to wait until Chapter 4 to try something. Grab a necklace, a shoelace with a key, or anything that swings. Rest your elbow on a table, let it dangle, and ask:

- "Show me, yes."
- "Show me, no."
- "Show me, maybe."

Watch what happens. Your pendulum just spoke. Welcome to the experiment.

What a Pendulum Is

(spoiler: it's not spooky, it's science + magic)

A pendulum is the simplest tool you'll ever own: a weight on a string. That's it. No batteries, no apps, no complicated instructions. You can buy one carved from amethyst or brass if you want—but honestly, your house is already full of pendulums-in-disguise. A necklace, a shoelace with a washer tied on, your earbuds dangling from the cord… boom. Instant pendulum.

So why does it feel like such a big deal? Because when it swings, it's not just moving—it's responding to *you*.

Scientists will tell you it's your body making tiny, unconscious movements (they call this the **ideomotor effect**). Your brain sends little signals you don't even notice, and your fingers pass them down the chain. That's the **science** part.

But here's the **magic** part: those micro-movements come from deep inside—your subconscious mind, your intuition, your "gut." Some people say it's your higher self or your energy field answering. Others call it tapping into universal wisdom. Either way, your pendulum is basically a translator between your inner knowing and the outside world.

Think of it like this:

- Your mind is Google.
- Your pendulum is the search bar.
- Together, they pull up answers you didn't even realize you had stored.

And no—it's not spooky. It's not summoning ghosts, casting spells, or unlocking portals (unless you decide to go there later).

At its core, pendulum work is just you having a conversation with… well, *you.*

EVERYDAY PENDULUMS YOU ALREADY KNOW

You've actually been around pendulums your whole life—you just didn't call them that.

- **Grandfather clocks:** That steady "tick-tock" is a pendulum swinging back and forth, keeping perfect time. Without pendulums, we wouldn't have had accurate clocks for centuries.

- **Newton's Cradle (the ball-on-string desk toy):** Tap one ball, and the energy swings through the others until the ball on the opposite side flies out. That's pure pendulum physics—energy transferring from one point to another.
- **Playground swings:** Yep, every time you swing back and forth, you're basically a giant human pendulum. Gravity and momentum keep you moving.
- **Wrecking balls:** Okay, maybe you don't see these every day, but they're literally giant pendulums with destructive power.

So, pendulums aren't rare, mystical objects hiding in dusty bookstores. They're part of daily life—controlling clocks, teaching physics, even showing up in your toys. The only difference is: *in this book, your pendulum isn't just about motion—it's about communication.*

YOUR FIRST "SWING TEST" EXPERIMENT

Okay, pause. Don't read this part too seriously. Just grab something that dangles—a necklace, a key on a string, even your earbuds. Hold it up so it can swing freely.

Now… just watch it.

Notice how even when you *think* you're holding your hand perfectly still, the pendulum starts to move. A tiny sway. A slow shift. A circle maybe. You didn't tell it to do that—at least not out loud.

Here's the curious part: if you silently *wonder* something, the swing changes. Ask in your head, *"Am I ready for this?"* or *"Will this thing actually work?"* Watch closely. It responds.

That's your first experiment. No instructions, no training—just you and a swinging object proving that something deeper is happening.

You don't have to believe in "energy" or "magic" yet. You just have to admit: this is interesting.

Chapter 1: Swing Thing

A Short History of Pendulums

(from Treasure Hunters to TikTok Witches)

Pendulums may feel new and mysterious, but humans have been fascinated by swinging objects for thousands of years. The difference? They weren't always using them to decide whether to text someone back.

ANCIENT TREASURE HUNTERS

Long before Google Maps or drilling rigs, people were trying to find water, minerals, and even treasure. They discovered that a forked stick—or later, a small pendulum—would start to twitch when held over hidden springs or metal veins. This practice became known as **dowsing**.

- In ancient China, texts mention "divining rods" used to locate water.
- In Europe, miners in the Middle Ages swore by their pendulums to find ore veins.
- Some even risked punishment from the Church for "witchcraft" because their methods seemed too uncanny to be natural.

Whether you believe it was intuition, sensitivity to the earth's magnetic field, or something else, the fact is: pendulums have been part of human survival for centuries.

SCIENTISTS GOT INVOLVED TOO

By the 1600s, pendulums were no longer just mystical tools—
they were the backbone of science. Galileo studied swinging
chandeliers and realized pendulums could measure time. That
led to the invention of the **pendulum clock**, which gave us the
most accurate timekeeping the world had ever known. For over
300 years, pendulum clocks ruled before quartz and digital took
over.

Even today, physics students study pendulums to learn about
gravity, motion, and resonance. In other words: pendulums are
not just "woo-woo." They're also the stuff of hard science.

SPIRITUAL SEEKERS & HEALERS

By the 1800s and 1900s, pendulums swung back into spiritual
practice. Healers used them to test food, remedies, and even the
human energy field. Some saw it as a way to bypass the logical
brain and tap into intuition. Others called it connecting to the
"higher self."

One famous modern pioneer was Hanna Kroeger, who taught
people to train their pendulum by tracing their hand, using it as
a kind of body-scanner to test health and energy.

FAST-FORWARD TO TIKTOK

Now, pendulums have made their way onto social media feeds.
Search "pendulum test" on TikTok, and you'll see teens holding
crystals over their hands, asking questions about relationships,
exams, or even what color to dye their hair. Some laugh it off as
a game; others treat it as guidance. Either way, the pendulum is
trending again—because honestly, who doesn't want a portable
decision-making tool that also looks cool on a chain?

WHY THIS HISTORY MATTERS

From treasure hunters to scientists, from spiritual healers to TikTok witches, pendulums have always walked the line between **practical tool** and **mystical symbol**. And now it's your turn to step into that story.

So the next time you dangle a necklace and it swings, remember: you're not just playing around—you're joining a tradition that's been swinging across centuries.

DID YOU KNOW? PENDULUM FUN FACTS

- **Galileo's Lamp:** The story goes that Galileo was in church, staring (bored) at a swinging chandelier. He noticed its swings were steady and predictable. That tiny observation led to the science of pendulums and, eventually, accurate clocks.
- **Courtroom Drama:** In the 1800s, some court cases in Europe actually tried to use pendulums as "truth detectors." (Spoiler: it didn't hold up in court, but people believed it for a while!)
- **Military Use:** During World War II, some soldiers used pendulums over maps to try and locate submarines or hidden enemy bases.
- **Sports Cheatsheet:** Athletes in the 1970s experimented with pendulums to test which foods or supplements improved performance.
- **TikTok Trend:** Millions of teens today post "pendulum tests" to see who likes them, which subject to study, or whether their vibes are "on point." It's basically the modern Magic 8-Ball—with more style.

Why Humans Love Moving Objects

Here's a weird fact about being human: we're wired to be fascinated by things that move on their own.

Think about it:

- Babies stare at mobiles dangling over their cribs.
- You can lose minutes (or hours) watching a campfire flicker.
- Lava lamps? Hypnotic.
- TikTok's "satisfying videos"? Same brain trick.

Pendulums hit that same button in our brains. They swing with a rhythm that feels both predictable *and* mysterious. We know it's gravity and momentum doing the work, but it *feels* like something more.

Psychologists say our brains are built to notice patterns and movement because, way back when, it helped us survive. Spotting the swing of tall grass could mean a predator was nearby. Watching a bird's flight could mean food or danger. Movement grabs attention—and keeps it.

So when you stare at a pendulum, part of you is just enjoying the soothing, rhythmic motion. But another part—the curious, ancient part of your brain—is whispering: *"Wait… what's guiding it?"*

That's why pendulums feel both calming and mysterious. They pull on instincts as old as humanity itself.

Meet Your Pendulum: Anything That Dangles Can Work

Forget the idea that you need to buy some fancy crystal on a silver chain before you can start. A pendulum doesn't have to be expensive, mystical, or "official." It just has to swing.

Look around you right now—your house, your backpack, even your pocket is probably hiding a pendulum-in-disguise:

- A necklace with a charm on it
- A key on a shoelace
- Your earbuds dangling from the cord
- A string tied to a washer, paperclip, or even a Lego piece
- The zipper pull from your hoodie if you tilt it just right

If it dangles and moves freely, it counts.

Why? Because the power isn't in the object—it's in *you.* The pendulum is just a translator, swinging in a way you can actually see what your body and subconscious are saying.

Sure, crystals are beautiful, and you'll eventually want to find one that feels special to you. But don't wait for the perfect pendulum to show up in a store. Start with what you have. Make it fun. Treat it like a secret superpower: you can turn almost anything into a pendulum and no one else even knows.

Chapter 2: Science, *But Fun*

The Ideomotor Effect: Your Brain's Secret Micro-Movements

Here's the thing: when your pendulum moves, it's not because ghosts are yanking the string or because the universe is bending physics just for you. The real MVP behind the scenes? **Your brain.**

Scientists call it the **ideomotor effect** (fancy word alert). What it means is: your brain sends tiny, invisible signals to your muscles—signals so small you don't even notice. These signals travel down your arm into your hand, and voilà… your pendulum swings.

It's like your body is whispering while your conscious mind is too busy talking.

Think of it this way:

- Ever started humming a song without realizing it was stuck in your head? That's your subconscious sneaking out.
- Ever reached for your phone before you even knew why? Same deal.
- Ever felt your foot tap along with music automatically? Yup—micro-movements.

The ideomotor effect proves that your body acts on thoughts, emotions, and questions *before you're even aware of it*. The pendulum is just the visual proof.

So no, it's not magic. But also—kind of yes, it is. Because your subconscious is basically a supercomputer running 24/7 beneath the surface. The pendulum lets you peek into its code.

Try This:

1. Hold your pendulum and silently think, *"Swing forward and back."*
   o Don't move your hand on purpose—just think it.
2. Now switch: *"Swing side to side."*
   o Watch how the swing changes, even though you didn't *try* to move it.
3. Next, tuck your elbow snugly into your side for extra support. Try again.
   o Notice how the swing is smaller, slower, or harder to start? That's because your body's micro-movements don't have as much room to sneak through when your arm is braced.

That's the ideomotor effect in action—your thoughts turning into invisible muscle signals, which turn into a visible pendulum swing.

Level Up Experiment: How Does Your Pendulum Behave?

You've seen how your thoughts alone can shift the pendulum. Now let's play with *conditions* to see what changes. Grab your pendulum and try each test below.

1. **Standing vs. Sitting**
   o Stand up, pendulum dangling. Ask it to swing "yes."
   o Now sit down, elbow on the table, and ask again.

     o   Which felt steadier? Which gave a bigger response?

2. **Eyes Open vs. Eyes Closed**
   - With eyes open, ask your pendulum a simple yes/no.
   - Close your eyes and repeat the same question.
   - Did the swing change when your vision wasn't guiding you?
3. **Elbow Free vs. Elbow Tucked**
   - Hold your pendulum with your elbow lifted and loose.
   - Then tuck your elbow tight against your side.
   - Which gave the stronger swing?
4. **Silly vs. Serious Questions**
   - Ask something obvious: "Is my name [your name]?"
   - Then ask something silly: "Do I live on Mars?"
   - Notice the difference in movement speed or confidence.

Journal It: Write down which conditions gave you the clearest results. This is how you start building trust with your pendulum—you're literally running your own experiments.

Tesla's Vibration Obsession (and Why He'd Be Into Pendulums)

Nikola Tesla, the brilliant inventor behind alternating current electricity, wireless experiments, and all kinds of futuristic ideas, once said:

"If you want to find the secrets of the universe, think in terms of energy, frequency, and vibration."

Tesla believed the entire universe was humming with invisible rhythms. He studied how sound waves could shatter glass, how electrical currents could create fields of energy, and how every single thing—rocks, plants, people—gives off a vibrational signature.

Now, guess what else is all about vibration and rhythm? Yep: pendulums.

- **A pendulum swings because of rhythm.** Gravity pulls it down, momentum carries it forward, and it repeats in a perfect cycle.
- **Your body's energy vibrates too.** When you hold a pendulum, your own micro-vibrations (from nerves, thoughts, even heartbeat) influence the swing.
- **Pendulums "tune in."** Just like Tesla tuned into frequencies, pendulums tune into the tiny shifts in your body and environment.

If Tesla were around today scrolling TikTok, he'd probably laugh at "pendulum challenges"—but secretly he'd geek out, because they show exactly what he preached: that vibration and energy are the hidden language of the universe.

So when your pendulum swings in response to a question, you're not just watching a weight dangle—you're seeing Tesla's theory in action: energy and frequency, made visible.

TESLA EXPERIMENT: FEEL THE VIBES

Tesla believed everything vibrates at its own frequency. You don't need a lab full of coils and lightning to test that—you can try it right now.

1. **Glass Tap Test**
   - Grab two drinking glasses (different sizes if possible).
   - Gently tap the rim with a spoon.

- o Notice how each one makes a different *ding*? That's their natural frequency.
2. **Water Trick**
   - o Fill one glass halfway with water. Tap again.
   - o Hear how the pitch is lower now? The water changed the vibration.
3. **Pendulum Connection**
   - o Hold your pendulum nearby.
   - o As you tap the glass, watch if the pendulum quivers or shifts slightly.
   - o Your pendulum, like Tesla, is tuning into vibration.

Think About It: If a glass of water can change its frequency, imagine how your own body—full of water, energy, and emotions—affects the swing of your pendulum.

EXPERIMENT: THE "MIND CONTROL" GAME

Before you learn how to actually program your pendulum to say *yes, no, maybe,* let's just play. Right now, your only job is to see how your thoughts make the swing change.

1. Hold your pendulum so it hangs freely.
2. In your mind, imagine it swinging forward and back. Really picture it.
3. Now switch—imagine it swinging side to side.
4. Try circles—first clockwise, then counterclockwise.

That's it. You're not asking questions or getting answers yet— you're just proving to yourself that your thoughts send micro-signals to your hand. You're not moving on purpose, but your brain is.

Challenge: Grab a friend. One of you thinks "forward/back" or "side/side," and the other tries to guess the thought by watching the pendulum. See who wins!

Chapter 3: Choose Your Vibe

Crystals, Coins, Paperclips, Shoelaces—Anything Goes

Here's the cool part: a pendulum doesn't have to be fancy. In fact, some of the best pendulums are the ones you make yourself out of whatever you've got lying around.

Sure, you'll see plenty of sparkly crystal pendulums for sale— rose quartz for love, amethyst for clarity, obsidian for protection. Those are beautiful and meaningful, and we'll get to them later. But for now? **Anything that dangles will do.**

- **Coins:** Tie a quarter, loonie, or euro coin to a string— instant pendulum.
- **Paperclips:** Hook one onto a thread or shoelace and let it swing.
- **Shoelaces:** Tie a bead, key, or even a Lego brick on the end.
- **Keys:** Your house key on a chain works like a charm (pun intended).
- **Necklaces:** Already wearing one? Boom. Pendulum unlocked.

Why this works: The object doesn't matter as much as *your connection to it*. Your pendulum is basically a swingy extension of your subconscious. The weight just gives your mind a way to make invisible micro-movements visible.

Quick Try:
Right now, find three different objects around you that could work as pendulums. Test them. Notice how each one feels in your hand. Is one lighter, faster, or more dramatic? Is one calmer or slower? Pick your favorite—that's your starter pendulum.

Make Your Own Pendulum

You don't have to spend money to get started. Yes, you can buy a pendulum (they come in every crystal and metal you can imagine), or you can keep it simple: a necklace works just fine. But if you want something that feels personal, try making your own.

You'll need:

- Thread or chain (gold or silver elastic thread works beautifully)
- Hot glue gun (or solder gun if you're comfortable using one)
- Beads (one large oblong bead, a metal or plastic cover, plus 3–5 smaller beads)

Procedure:

1. Cut a piece of thread about 10 inches long.
2. Attach one end of the thread to your large bead.
3. Slide a metal or plastic cover over the bead and thread.
4. Glue the pieces together securely.
5. String the smaller beads along the thread in any design you like.
6. Rest your elbow on a table and let the thread dangle.
7. Adjust so the large bead swings freely without touching the table.
8. Fold the top end of the thread at your fingertips.

9. Loop the folded end around and through to create a knot.
10. Pull tight.
11. Trim off the extra thread, leaving about ¼ inch above the knot.

That's it—you've just crafted your own pendulum!

Tip: The design doesn't matter as much as how it feels to you. Some people like sleek and simple; others decorate theirs with charms or colors that mean something. Your pendulum should be something you *want* to pick up and use.

How to Cleanse and "Sync" With Your Pendulum

Now that you've got a pendulum (whether you bought one, borrowed a necklace, or DIY'd your own craft project), it's time to **clear its energy** and make sure it's tuned in to *you*.

Think of it like pairing wireless earbuds—your pendulum works best when it's synced to your unique vibe.

Ways to Cleanse Your Pendulum:

- **Moonlight Bath:** Leave it on your windowsill overnight during a full moon.
- **Salt Rest:** Bury it in a small bowl of salt for a few hours to absorb old energy.
- **Smoke Cleanse:** Pass it through sage, incense, or even the steam from your favorite tea.
- **Crystal Recharge:** Place it on a piece of clear quartz or selenite.
- **Sound Vibes:** Play a singing bowl, tuning fork, or even a favorite playlist next to it.

How to Sync With Your Pendulum:

1. Hold it in your hands for a minute. Close your eyes.
2. Take a slow breath and imagine your energy flowing into it.
3. Whisper (or think): *"This pendulum works with me and only me."*
4. Carry it with you in your pocket or bag for a day so it "learns" your energy.

Pro Tip: If a friend asks to try your pendulum, that's fine—but always give it a quick cleanse afterward. Think of it as resetting your password.

PENDULUM PLAYLIST: CLEANSE WITH MUSIC

Who says cleansing has to be all incense and moonlight? Your pendulum vibes with *sound* just as much as you do. Try this:

1. Create a short playlist of 3–5 songs that feel like *you* right now. (Upbeat, calm, silly, dramatic—whatever fits your mood.)
2. Place your pendulum on the table or hold it gently while the playlist runs.
3. Imagine the music washing through it, clearing away old energy and syncing it with your personal vibe.
4. When the playlist ends, your pendulum is officially "tuned" to you.

Tip: Make a new playlist anytime you want a reset—like a "study vibes" pendulum playlist, or a "good energy only" one.

Extra Fun: Trade playlists with a friend, and see if your pendulum reacts differently to *their* vibe versus yours.

Chapter 4: Teach It to Talk

Yes, No, Maybe Signals

Your pendulum is ready. It's clean, synced, and swinging. But before you can start asking real questions, you need to agree on one thing: **How does it say "yes," "no," and "maybe"?**

Think of it like learning a new language. Every pendulum has its own "accent," and every person has their own way of receiving signals. Your job now is to figure out your pendulum's style.

Step 1: Meet Your "Yes"

- Hold your pendulum with your elbow resting on a table.
- Take a deep breath and ask (silently or out loud): *"Pendulum, please show me yes."*
- Wait. Watch. It might swing forward and back, side to side, or even in a diagonal line.
- Don't overthink—whatever it does first, that's your yes.

Step 2: Meet Your "No"

- Reset your pendulum by holding it still for a moment.
- Ask: *"Pendulum, please show me no."*
- Again, watch what happens. It will usually swing in a different direction.

Step 3: The "Maybe" (or "Not Now")

- Ask: *"Pendulum, please show me maybe."*
- Often this comes as a circle, a wobble, or a tiny swing that doesn't commit.
- Think of "maybe" as your pendulum's way of saying: *"Ask again later, the vibes aren't clear."*

Step 4: Double-Check

Ask a question you already know the answer to, like:

- *"Is my name [your name]?"* (should give you a yes)
- *"Do I live on Mars?"* (should give you a no)

If the answers line up, congrats—you've just learned your pendulum's language!

Pro Tip: Don't worry if your signals change over time. Some pendulums start with one pattern and evolve as your connection deepens. Just check in every so often to confirm.

WANT TO SEE IT IN ACTION?

Reading is one thing—but sometimes you need to *see* this in real life. I've made a short video where I walk you through the steps, show you what the sways look like, and give you extra tips for getting clear results.

Watch it here: https://youtu.be/SHkYd9vgeuI

The Hanna Kroeger Method: The Hand Test

Want another way to program your pendulum? This method comes from Hanna Kroeger, a well-known healer who taught people to use the body itself as a guide. It's simple, visual, and surprisingly powerful.

What to Do:

1. Place your hand flat on a table.
2. On a sheet of paper, trace the outline of your hand.
3. Hold your pendulum over the drawing, starting with the **middle finger nail**.
   - Ask: *"Pendulum, show me yes."*
   - Watch the swing. Repeat the request until the pendulum always moves in the same direction, even if you stop and restart.
   - This finger becomes your **positive polarity** (your "yes").
4. Move to the **pointer finger nail**.
   - Ask: *"Pendulum, show me no."*
   - Again, repeat until the pendulum consistently swings the same way.
   - This finger becomes your **negative polarity** (your "no").
5. Finally, move to the **thumbnail**.
   - Ask: *"Pendulum, show me neutral" or *Show me: ask a better question."*
   - Repeat until the movement is steady and reliable.
   - This finger becomes your **neutral polarity** (your "maybe" or "not now").

Why This Works:
Your body already carries polarity—positive, negative, neutral—just like a battery. By using your hand as a "map,"

you're giving your pendulum a clear framework to follow. It's like teaching it the rules of the game before you play.

Pro Tip: Save your hand tracing in a journal. Over time, you can use it as a quick calibration tool whenever you want to re-check or reset your pendulum's signals.

WANT TO SEE IT IN ACTION?

Reading is one thing—but sometimes you need to *see* the hand pendulum in real life. I've made a short video where I walk you through the steps, show you what the sways look like, and give you extra tips for getting clear results.

Watch it here: https://youtu.be/FNd3pPvLsio

PRACTICE MAKES PATTERNS

Here's the secret: don't expect your pendulum to give perfect, identical signals the first time. Like any language, it takes repetition. Keep asking, keep pausing, and keep restarting until the movement for each finger is always the same.

For some people, this "clicks" in just a few minutes. For others, it takes hours, days, weeks—or even months. And that's okay. You're not doing it wrong. You're training your pendulum *and* yourself to communicate consistently.

The goal isn't speed—it's trust. Once your pendulum's signals are steady, you'll never doubt whether it's saying yes, no, or neutral again.

FRUSTRATION FIXES: WHEN YOUR PENDULUM WON'T PLAY ALONG

Don't panic if your pendulum feels stubborn or confusing at first. Here are quick resets you can try:

- **Ground Yourself:** Take three deep breaths, put both feet flat on the floor, and relax your shoulders. A calm body = clearer signals.
- **Cleanse It:** Pass your pendulum through incense smoke, set it on a piece of clear quartz, or give it a quick moonlight recharge.
- **Reset Your Space:** Turn off distractions—TV, phone notifications, background chatter—pendulums like focused vibes.
- **Switch Hands:** If it's not working in your dominant hand, try the other one. Sometimes the connection is stronger.
- **Take a Break:** Walk away for 10 minutes (or even a day). When you come back fresh, your pendulum may behave differently.

- **Check Your Questions:** Make sure you're asking simple yes/no questions. Complicated or emotional ones can muddy the swing.

Reminder: Struggle doesn't mean failure—it means you're learning. Pendulum communication is like tuning a radio. Sometimes you just have to adjust the dial until the station comes in clearly.

QUICK PRACTICE: SILLY VS. SERIOUS QUESTIONS

Now that your pendulum has shown you its yes/no/maybe moves, it's time to test-drive it. The trick? Start with questions you *already know the answers to*.

Try This: Pendulum Practice Round

1. **Start with the Obvious (Serious "Yes" Questions):**
   Ask things you already know are true. Your pendulum should give you a clear **yes**.
   - *"Is my name [insert your name]?"*
   - *"Am I holding a pendulum?"*
   - *"Do I live on planet Earth?"*
   - *"Is the sky above me right now?"*
   - *"Am I reading this book?"*
2. **Test the Opposite (Serious "No" Questions):**
   Ask questions where the answer is definitely no. Your pendulum should swing in your **no** direction.
   - *"Am I a banana?"*
   - *"Is my best friend an alien in disguise?"*
   - *"Do I live on Mars?"*
   - *"Is water dry?"*
   - *"Do unicorns deliver the mail?"*
3. **Silly Fun Round (Ridiculous Questions):**
   Time to get playful! Watch how strongly your pendulum reacts when the question is silly.
   - *"Do I secretly have three heads?"*

- o *"Is pizza made out of clouds?"*
- o *"Do cows sing opera when humans aren't looking?"*
- o *"Will my math homework do itself if I stare at it long enough?"*
- o *"Am I secretly a superhero in disguise?"*

4. **Wild Cards (Unanswerable or Open-Ended):**
   These are the "maybe," "not now," or *"ask a better question"* signals.
   - o *"Will I marry a movie star?"*
   - o *"Will my dog ever learn to talk?"*
   - o *"Will my crush text me today?"*
   - o *"Will I win the lottery before I'm 20?"*
   - o *"Will school ever be canceled forever?"*

5. **Friend Flip Game (If you're practicing with someone else):**
   - o Have a friend ask you silly/serious/wild questions while you hold the pendulum.
   - o You can even swap: you ask questions and let *them* hold the pendulum.
   - o Compare results—do your pendulums give the same "vibes" or different ones?

The point isn't whether the answers are *true* yet—it's about building muscle memory between you and your pendulum. Silly questions keep it lighthearted, serious ones build consistency, and wild cards teach you how to recognize a "not now" swing.

Why Do This?
These practice rounds train your pendulum (and your brain) to lock in its signals. Plus, starting with low-stakes, funny questions takes the pressure off. You're building trust without overthinking.

Pro Tip: Write down your pendulum's answers in a journal—even the goofy ones. Over time, you'll see your swings get stronger, faster, and more consistent.

The Pendulum and Literal Questions

Here's the thing about your pendulum: it's not vague, magical, or poetic. It's **literal**. It answers the exact words you use—not what you *meant* to ask.

Okay, real talk: your pendulum is *literal.* Like, painfully literal. It doesn't do sarcasm, it doesn't guess what you "meant," and it definitely doesn't read between the lines. If your question is fuzzy, your answer will be fuzzy too.

Think of your pendulum like a computer. If you type in garbage, it spits out garbage. But if you type in exactly what you want, you'll get a clear result. Or think of your subconscious mind like a super-smart robot. It doesn't "guess" or "interpret." It just responds to the question exactly as you frame it. If your question is sloppy, your answer will be too.

❌ Fuzzy Question vs ✅ Clear Question

❌ *"Should I move?"*
→ Move where? When? To the couch? To another city? Too vague.

✅ *"Is it in my best interest to move to [insert city] this year?"*
→ That's clear. One location. One timeframe. Your pendulum can handle that.

❌ *"Does my body like this food?"*
→ "Like" is emotional. Your body doesn't "like" Doritos—it either gets energy from them or it crashes.

✅ *"Will this food support my body's energy right now?"*
→ Clear, literal, answerable.

❌ *"Will my crush text me back?"*

→ That's out of your control. Your pendulum doesn't hack other people's free will.

✅ *"Is it in my best interest to text [crush's name] today?"*

→ Now it's about *you*. The pendulum is basically helping you decide if it's worth pressing send.

Tips for Asking Like a Pro

- **One thing at a time.** Don't pile on: *"Should I study tonight or tomorrow and also clean my room?"* Pick one question.
- **Stay in the now.** Say "today" or "right now." Don't ask forever-questions like *"Will I ever be famous?"* (your pendulum is not TikTok's algorithm).
- **Skip drama words.** Words like "love," "want," or "maybe" are too loaded. Stick to neutral, measurable ones like "support," "help," or "align."
- **Keep it literal.** If you text the pendulum like you text your BFF—half sentences, emojis, vague hints—it won't work. The pendulum isn't your bestie; it's your subconscious. Spell it out.

Pro Tip: If your pendulum goes in circles, freezes, or just feels "off," it's not broken—it's telling you, *"Ask a better question."*

Chapter 5: Your Body's Secret Lie Detector

The Body Pendulum: Sway Forward, Sway Back

Here's something wild: you don't always need an object on a string to use pendulum energy. Your **whole body** can act like a pendulum. That's right—you are the pendulum.

How It Works

Just like with a handheld pendulum, your subconscious sends tiny signals through your body. When you stand still, those signals can show up as gentle sways forward, backward, or even side to side. Your body becomes the "swing" while gravity and balance do the rest.

It's simple, sneaky, and incredibly accurate once you get the hang of it.

Step 1: Train the Motion

- Stand with your feet hip-width apart.
- Keep your knees relaxed—not locked tight, but not wobbly either.
- Imagine you're a stiff two-by-four from your ankles up.
- Now lean forward slightly and say: *"Forward without falling is YES."*
- Lean back slightly and say: *"Backward without falling is NO."*
- Repeat this three times to lock it into your body.

Step 2: Practice with High-Vibe Objects

Vitamins are perfect for practice because they carry such a high vibratory rate.

- Hold a bottle of vitamins against your stomach.
- Ask: *"Is this vitamin what my body needs today?"*
- Relax. Let your body move naturally.
  - If you sway **forward**, that's a yes.
  - If you sway **backward**, that's a no.
  - If you go **side to side**, it means the question is unclear—try asking it in a more specific way.

Step 3: Build Confidence

- Try this with 5–10 different kinds of vitamins.
- Once you can clearly feel the difference between yes and no, switch it up:
  - Hold a piece of candy. Ask, *"Does my body need this today?"*
  - Ask, *"Is my name [insert your name] in this lifetime?"*
  - Play with other true/false questions that have only one possible answer.

Step 4: Get Specific

This tool only works for **yes/no questions**—so be crystal clear.

- Example: After a dream, I once asked: *"Should I move the school?"* My body pendulum said **no**.
- Then I asked: *"Should I move all the contents of the school?"* My body pendulum said **yes**.
- The answer was literal: the school building (bricks and wood) should stay—but the furniture and supplies should be moved.

Step 5: A Note on Honesty

- Always ask for an **honest and unbiased answer.**
- Sometimes your conscious mind already knows what it *wants* the answer to be—and that can interfere.
- If you're practicing on a client, they can simply *think* the question, while you test with your body pendulum. This is also a great way to discover a person's natural **channel of communication** (how they best receive truth).

Why It Works

Your subconscious knows the truth. When you ask a question, your nervous system reacts instantly—faster than your thinking mind. Muscles tighten or relax, breath shifts, and your body subtly leans. The body pendulum turns those micro-responses into movement you can actually feel.

Pro Tip: The more specific the question, the clearer the answer. Vague questions confuse the body pendulum—your subconscious is literal, like a very smart robot.

If your sways feel too small, try it barefoot on a hard floor with your hands resting loosely at your sides. The less tension in your body, the clearer the response.

WANT TO SEE IT IN ACTION?

Reading is one thing—but sometimes you need to *see* this in real life. I've made a short video where I walk you through the steps, show you what the sways look like, and give you extra tips for getting clear results.

Watch it here: https://youtu.be/VPILG41aAeA

The Finger Lock Test: Strength Check

Here's another way to tap into your body's hidden truth signals—this time using just your hands. The **Finger Lock Test** is quick, subtle, and super portable. You can do it under a desk, at a café, or even while waiting in line. No one will know you're basically running a lie detector test on yourself.

Step 1: Make the Lock

- Touch the tip of your **thumb** and **pointer finger** together to form a circle.
- Think of this circle as a "lock."

Step 2: Add the Key

- With your other hand, make the same lock.
- Slip one circle inside the other, like two chain links.

Step 3: Test "Yes"

- Ask your body to show you a **yes.**
- Try to pull the circles apart by gently tugging.
- A true "yes" usually feels **stronger**—your fingers resist opening.

Step 4: Test "No"

- Reset and ask for a **no.**
- Try pulling the circles apart again.
- A true "no" usually feels **weaker**—the lock breaks open more easily.

Step 5: Practice Questions

- Ask: *"Is my name [insert name]?"* → should hold strong.
- Ask: *"Do I live on Mars?"* → should break apart.
- Ask: *"Do I need water right now?"* → notice the subtle difference.

Why It Works:

Your body's muscles subtly respond to stress, truth, or resonance. When something aligns with your subconscious truth, you feel stronger. When it doesn't, your body weakens slightly. The finger lock makes that difference easy to see.

The Infinity Finger Test

If you like the Finger Lock Test, here's its stylish cousin—the **Infinity Finger Test**. This one is quick, subtle, and shaped like the infinity symbol (∞). You only need two fingers from each hand, and it's easy to do anywhere.

Step 1: Make the Loops

- With your **right hand**, touch your thumb and pointer finger together to make a circle.
- Do the same with your **left hand**.

Step 2: Link Them

- Slide one loop through the other so they look like a sideways figure eight, or infinity symbol.

Step 3: Program "Yes" and "No"

- Ask your body: *"Show me yes."*
- Gently pull your hands apart. If "yes," the loops usually hold strong.
- Reset, then ask: *"Show me no."*
- This time, your fingers often slip apart more easily.

Step 4: Play With It

- Ask a simple truth: *"Is my name [insert your name]?"* → should hold strong.
- Ask something silly: *"Do I live on Jupiter?"* → should break open.
- Ask a personal check-in: *"Does my body need more water right now?"* → notice the difference.

Why It Works:
Just like the regular Finger Lock Test, your subconscious subtly strengthens or weakens your muscles depending on truth or stress. The infinity shape makes the movement smooth and easy to feel.

The Classic Arm Test: Partner Practice

This is the classic way muscle testing has been taught for decades—and it's best done with a partner. Instead of watching a pendulum swing, you're testing how strong (or weak) your arm feels in response to a yes/no question. It's simple, but surprisingly powerful.

Step 1: Get Into Position

- Stand tall with your feet hip-width apart.
- Relax your shoulders and breathe normally.
- Extend one arm straight out to the side, palm down.

Step 2: Ask a Clear Question

- Think of something true: *"Is my name [insert your name]?"*
- Or false: *"Is my name SpongeBob?"*
- Keep it simple—only yes/no questions work.

Step 3: Apply Gentle Pressure

- Have your partner place two fingers on your extended arm, just above the wrist.
- They should gently push downward while you resist— not a wrestling match, just steady pressure.

Step 4: Notice the Response

- On a true/"yes," your arm usually holds strong and resists easily.
- On a false/"no," your arm often feels weaker—it dips slightly, or you can't resist as firmly.

Step 5: Practice Rounds

Try a mix of questions:

- *"Do I live on Earth?"* (yes = strong)
- *"Am I a dolphin?"* (no = weak)
- Hold a food or vitamin to your chest and ask: *"Is this good for me today?"*
- Switch partners and let them try too.

Why It Works:
Your nervous system reacts instantly to truth or stress. When something is in harmony with you, muscles stay strong. When something isn't, they weaken—just enough for you to notice.

Tip: This works best with trust. Your partner should use light, steady pressure—not try to "win."

WANT TO SEE IT IN ACTION?

Reading is one thing—but sometimes you need to *see* this in real life. I've made a short video where I walk you through the steps, show you what the sways look like, and give you extra tips for getting clear results.

Watch it here: https://youtu.be/8kIQIcAwBs0

PARTNER CHALLENGE: TRUTH VS. TEST

Grab a friend or family member and turn the Classic Arm Test into a game. The goal isn't to "beat" each other—it's to notice how the body reacts differently depending on the question or object.

Round 1: Obvious Questions

- Ask: *"Is your name [real name]?"* → strong.
- Ask: *"Is your name Batman?"* → weak.
- Ask: *"Do you live on planet Earth?"* → strong.

Round 2: Food & Drink

- Hold a vitamin or a bottle of water to your chest. Ask: *"Is this good for me right now?"*
- Now try it with candy, soda, or chips. Notice how the arm often weakens.

Round 3: Mystery Objects

- Close your eyes. Have your partner hand you two different items (a crystal, phone, snack, pencil).
- Hold each one to your chest while they ask: *"Is this good for my energy today?"*
- See if you can tell which item your body prefers just from the arm test.

Round 4: Switch Roles

- Let your partner hold out their arm while you apply gentle pressure.
- Compare notes. Do you both get similar results?

Reminder: This test works best when both people stay relaxed and curious. Think of it as a science experiment, not a contest.

WHEN TO USE MUSCLE TESTING VS. PENDULUM

Both pendulums and muscle testing tap into the same thing—your subconscious truth signals. The difference is in **how** you get the answers. Think of them as two apps on the same phone. Sometimes you use one, sometimes the other.

Use Muscle Testing When...

- You want something **quick and subtle** (like the Finger Lock Test under a desk).
- You don't have a pendulum handy.
- You're checking **physical alignment**—foods, vitamins, drinks, supplements.
- You're working with a **partner or client** and want interactive feedback.
- You need to cut through your mind's chatter—muscles often respond faster than you expect.

Use a Pendulum When...

- You want a **visual answer**—watching the swing helps build trust.
- You're exploring **energy fields, chakras, or aura checks.**
- You're doing **map dowsing, treasure hunting, or decision grids.**
- You enjoy ritual—cleansing, syncing, and setting intention.
- You want to go deeper into **spiritual questions or intuition training.**

Pro Tip: You don't have to choose just one. Many people use muscle testing for **body-based decisions** (what to eat, take, or avoid) and pendulums for **life-based questions** (what direction to move in, what's aligned with their energy). Both are tools. The real power is in you.

Chapter 6: Everyday Magic

Should I Eat This? (Teens: Snacks; Adults: Supplements)

Your pendulum isn't just a "yes/no toy." It can be a surprisingly useful tool for daily decisions—like figuring out what your body actually wants (and doesn't want) to eat.

How It Works

Every food, drink, or supplement carries its own vibrational "signature." Your body knows what helps it thrive and what drags it down. A pendulum lets you tap into that wisdom quickly and visually.

Try It With Snacks

Grab two snacks—maybe chips and an apple.

1. Hold one in your hand or place it on the table.
2. Hover your pendulum over it and ask:
   o *"Is this snack good for my body right now?"*
3. Watch the swing. Forward/back might be yes, side-to-side might be no.
4. Repeat with the other snack. Compare the answers.

Fun Twist: Ask your pendulum to pick between pizza toppings, your favorite drink, or even which candy you should have. (It doesn't mean you *can't* eat candy—it just shows you what your body's vibing with in the moment.)

Try It With Supplements

1. Hold the vitamin or supplement bottle near your stomach or heart.
2. Hover your pendulum over your hand holding the bottle.
3. Ask: *"Does my body need this supplement today?"*
4. Let the pendulum swing. A strong yes means supportive; a no means maybe skip it.

Pro Tip: Even healthy things aren't always right for you in every moment. Your pendulum can help you fine-tune what your body actually needs each day.

Your conscious mind might crave sugar or assume you "should" take every supplement in your cupboard. But your subconscious body wisdom is literal and honest. A pendulum cuts through cravings, trends, and guesswork to give you an instant check-in.

PENDULUM FOOD JOURNAL EXERCISE

Your pendulum is giving you signals—but the real test is how you *feel* after you eat or drink. Use this journal exercise to track both, and you'll start noticing patterns quickly.

Step 1: Before eating, test your food or supplement with your pendulum.
Step 2: Write down what you tested and what answer you got (Yes, No, Maybe).
Step 3: After eating/drinking, note how your body feels 30–60 minutes later. Energized? Sleepy? Balanced? Bloated? Clear?

Sample Journal Page

Date	Food / Drink / Supplement	Pendulum Answer	How I Felt After	Notes
Sept 22	Apple	Yes	Energized, focused	Great study snack
Sept 22	Soda	No	Jittery, then tired	Confirmed what the pendulum said
Sept 23	Multivitamin	Yes	Steady energy all morning	Good choice
Sept 23	Candy bar	Maybe	Quick sugar rush, then crash	Next time, a smaller piece

Why This Works:

Your pendulum gives the immediate yes/no, but your journal shows the bigger picture. Over time, you'll build a personal "food wisdom guide" based on both pendulum responses *and* your lived experience.

TWEEN TWIST: SNACK NIGHT CHALLENGE

Pendulums aren't just for deep questions—you can turn them into a fun game with friends.

Here's how:

1. Before movie night, each person tests their snacks with their pendulum.
   - Chips? Candy? Popcorn? Energy drinks?
   - Ask: *"Is this snack good for my body right now?"*

2. Everyone writes down their pendulum answers (Yes, No, Maybe).
3. Dig in anyway (because duh—it's movie night).
4. After the movie, compare notes. Who got sleepy? Who stayed energized? Who got the sugar crash?

The Lesson: Your pendulum is like your body's spoiler alert. It often knows how you'll feel before you even take the first bite.

Decision Roulette (What Outfit? What Job?)

Ever get stuck in the *ugh* zone—standing in front of your closet wondering what to wear, or staring at two big life options thinking, *How am I supposed to choose?* Your pendulum can help you cut through the overthinking.

Step 1: Set Up the Choices

- Write each option on a small piece of paper (Outfit A / Outfit B, Job 1 / Job 2, etc.).
- Place them in front of you in a line or circle.

Step 2: Call In the Pendulum

- Hold your pendulum over the first option.
- Ask: *"Is this the best choice for me right now?"*
- Note the swing—yes, no, or maybe.

Step 3: Compare Results

- Move to the next option and ask the same question.
- Work through all your choices.
- The pendulum usually gives you a clear favorite.

Step 4: The Spin Game (Roulette Style)

If you want to make it more fun:

1. Place all your options in a circle.
2. Hold the pendulum in the center and ask: *"Which option is most aligned with me today?"*
3. Let the pendulum swing toward the winning choice.

Tip for Teens: Try it with outfits, nail polish colors, or even "Which TikTok should I post today?"
Tip for Adults: Use it for bigger decisions like "Which job offer?" or "Should I apply for this program?"

Important: Your pendulum gives insight, but it doesn't replace common sense. Always double-check that the choice makes sense in real life too.

Lost & Found Game (Keys, Phone, AirPods)

We've all been there—you're late, your bag is upside down, and your keys are hiding like they're in witness protection. Good news: your pendulum can double as a personal "find it" tool.

Step 1: Narrow the Search

- Start by asking broad questions:
    - *"Are my keys in the house?"*
    - *"Are they in the car?"*
    - *"Are they outside?"*
- The pendulum's yes/no answers help you rule out whole areas.

Step 2: Zone In

- Once you know the general location, stand in the room.
- Hold the pendulum and ask: *"Are my keys in this room?"*
- Keep moving until you get a clear yes.

Step 3: Hot or Cold

- Walk slowly around the room with your pendulum dangling in front of you.
- When you're close to the object, the pendulum often swings faster, stronger, or points toward it.

Step 4: Test on a Map

- If you're really stuck, draw a quick map of your house or room.
- Hover the pendulum over different areas and ask: *"Are my keys here?"*
- Let it guide you like a treasure map.

Pro Tip: Start with smaller, playful searches. Hide an item (like a coin) with a friend and use your pendulum to find it. The more you practice, the more accurate your "lost & found radar" becomes.

Heads Up: Your pendulum won't magically beam AirPods out of the couch cushions—it just helps your subconscious remember where you last saw them. Think of it as a memory booster, not X-ray vision.

Chapter 7: Pendulum Treasure Hunt

The Ancient Art of Water Dowsing

Long before plumbing, city maps, or bottled water, people had one big problem: *where the heck do we dig to find water?* Enter: the dowser.

For thousands of years, people used sticks, rods, and later pendulums to locate underground springs. This practice is called **water dowsing** (or sometimes "water witching"). The dowser would walk across land holding a Y-shaped branch or pendulum, asking silently for the location of water. When they passed over a hidden source, the tool would twitch, dip, or swing as if pulled by invisible hands.

A Quick Trip Through History

- **Ancient China (around 2000 BCE):** Writings mention the use of wooden rods to locate underground water.
- **Medieval Europe:** Miners used pendulums and rods to find not just water, but also veins of silver, gold, and other minerals.
- **Early America:** Farmers often hired dowsers with forked sticks to find the best spots to dig wells.

Some thought it was a gift. Others thought it was witchcraft. Skeptics said it was imagination. But here's the truth: dowsing has been around *forever*, because—whether you call it science, intuition, or magic—it often worked.

How It Might Work

Scientists argue the ideomotor effect is still at play: your body senses subtle environmental clues (like changes in humidity, soil density, or energy fields) and passes that info to your tool. You don't notice, but your subconscious does. The pendulum makes it visible.

Fun Fact: In the 20th century, some military units even experimented with map dowsing to find water supplies in remote locations.

TRY IT YOURSELF: MINI WATER DOWSING GAME

Ready to play dowser for a day? You don't need acres of farmland—you can practice inside with a simple setup.

What You'll Need

- 3–5 small boxes, cups, or bowls (not see-through).
- One bottle or glass filled with water.
- A pendulum.
- A friend to help set it up (optional, but makes it more fun).

Step 1: Hide the Water

- Place the bottle of water under one of the boxes.
- Shuffle them around so you (or your partner) doesn't know which one it's under.

Step 2: Ask the Question

- Hold your pendulum over the first box and ask: *"Is the water under this one?"*
- Watch for your yes/no signal.

Step 3: Check Each Box

- Move slowly across the boxes, asking the same question.
- The pendulum should swing strongest over the water.

Step 4: Reveal the Answer

- Once you've picked the box, lift it up and see if your pendulum was right.

Variation: If you're playing with friends, take turns hiding the water and dowsing. Keep score to see who gets the most hits.

Why This Works: Your body might be picking up subtle clues—like temperature, condensation, or just intuitive "knowing." The pendulum makes those subconscious signals visible.

MAP DOWSING CHALLENGE WITH FRIENDS

You don't need a field and a shovel to try water dowsing—you can turn it into a fun game right at home. All you need is a map (or a quick sketch).

Step 1: Make Your Map

- Draw a simple map of your house, backyard, school, or neighborhood.
- Keep it basic—just blocks, rooms, or zones.

Step 2: Pick the "Treasure"

- Decide what you're "searching" for. It could be:
  - A hidden bottle of water (to mimic real dowsing).
  - A snack someone stashed.

- o Even a mystery location one person chooses but doesn't tell the group.

Step 3: Dowse the Map

- Each player hovers their pendulum over the map and asks:
  "Is the treasure here?"
- Move slowly across zones until the pendulum swings a strong yes.

Step 4: Test It in Real Life

- Once you've marked your "X" on the map, go check the spot in person.
- Did your pendulum point to the right area?

Step 5: Swap Roles

- Let someone else hide the treasure while the others dowse.
- Keep score for bragging rights!

Pro Tip: This practice sharpens your pendulum skills. Even if you're not hunting actual water, you're training your subconscious to notice patterns and tune into energy.

Everyday Magic: Top 10 Fast Uses for Your Pendulum

1. **Snack Check:** *"Is this food good for my body right now?"*
2. **Drink Test:** Water vs. soda, coffee vs. tea—see what your body wants.
3. **Supplement Check:** *"Do I need this vitamin today?"*
4. **Outfit Vibes:** Hold up two outfits and ask, *"Which matches my energy today?"*
5. **Homework/Study Order:** *"Should I start with math or English?"*
6. **Lost & Found:** Hover your pendulum over a map, floor plan, or even a messy bedroom to find missing items.
7. **Movie/Game Night:** Let the pendulum pick between options when no one can agree.
8. **Music Mood:** Hover over your playlist or shuffle songs—let your pendulum choose the vibe.
9. **Daily Check-In:** Ask, *"Do I need more rest today?"* or *"Is exercise what my body needs?"*
10. **Quick Clarity:** When your brain feels foggy, ask one yes/no question to reset.

Pro Tip: Keep your pendulum somewhere easy to grab—like your pocket, backpack, or nightstand. The more you use it in everyday choices, the stronger (and faster) your connection grows.

Earth's Hidden Magnetic Fields

Here's something cool: your pendulum isn't just swinging in empty space—it's moving inside Earth's invisible web of **magnetic fields.**

The Earth is basically one giant magnet. Deep inside, molten iron is spinning, creating magnetic currents that stretch all the way around the globe. This is why compasses point north and why birds can migrate thousands of miles without getting lost.

So How Does This Connect to Pendulums?

- When you hold a pendulum, you're not only tapping into your subconscious—you're also standing in Earth's natural energy field.
- Water flowing underground, metal veins in the earth, even electrical wires in your walls all give off subtle electromagnetic signals.
- Some scientists believe dowsers (people who use rods or pendulums) may be subconsciously sensitive to these shifts. Their bodies pick it up, and the pendulum swings in response.

Try This: Compass + Pendulum

1. Grab a simple compass and notice where north is.
2. Stand in that direction, then hold your pendulum still.
3. Ask: *"Show me yes."* Notice the swing.
4. Now turn east, south, and west. Does the pendulum feel stronger or weaker in certain directions?

Even if you don't "prove" anything scientific, you're experimenting with how your pendulum might interact with the planet's natural rhythms.

Fun Fact: Ancient builders (like in Stonehenge or the Great Pyramids) often placed their monuments along powerful energy lines. Some dowsers claim pendulums can detect those same lines today.

PENDULUM CHALLENGE: BE A MODERN DOWSER

For centuries, people used pendulums to find water, minerals, or even lost treasure. You don't need a shovel or a field to try it—you can do it right now with your phone.

Step 1: Open the maps app on your phone (Google Maps, Apple Maps—whatever you use). Zoom in on your city or neighborhood.

Step 2: Hold your pendulum above the screen. Ask it:

- *"Show me where I should go explore."*
- *"Point me to a place with good energy."*
- *"Where would I have the most fun today?"*

Step 3: Notice where it swings. Maybe toward the park, your favorite café, or some random spot you've never been.

Step 4: If you're feeling adventurous, actually go there—or make a note of it in your journal to test later.

Pro Tip: In history, dowsers would mark spots on maps where their pendulums swung strongest, then send crews to dig wells or mines. You don't have to dig up your backyard (your parents will thank me), but you can use this to let curiosity guide you somewhere new.

Chapter 8: Energy & Vibes

Scan Your Aura and Chakras

Your pendulum isn't just for yes/no questions or treasure hunts—it can also check in on your personal energy field. Think of it as a vibe detector, showing you where energy flows smoothly and where it might feel blocked.

What's an Aura?

Your **aura** is the energy bubble around you. Some describe it as light, others as a field of vibration. You don't have to "see" it to believe it—your pendulum can sense it for you.

What Are Chakras?

Chakras are like energy hubs in your body. Picture them as spinning wheels that help keep you balanced physically, emotionally, and spiritually. There are seven main chakras, running from the base of your spine to the top of your head:

1. Root (safety & stability)
2. Sacral (creativity & emotions)
3. Solar Plexus (confidence & power)
4. Heart (love & compassion)
5. Throat (communication & truth)
6. Third Eye (intuition & insight)
7. Crown (connection & spirit)

How to Scan Your Aura

1. Stand or sit comfortably.
2. Hold your pendulum a few inches away from your body—start near your hand or shoulder.
3. Slowly move it outward, away from your body.
4. Watch when the pendulum starts to swing—it's sensing your energy field.

Try this with a friend: stand still while they scan your aura with a pendulum. Compare results—do you both notice the same "edge" of the energy bubble?

WANT TO SEE IT IN ACTION?

Reading is one thing—but sometimes you need to *see* the body pendulum in real life. I've made a short video where I walk you through the steps, show you what the sways look like, and give you extra tips for getting clear results.

Watch it here: https://youtu.be/eE1zFHFrGjE and https://youtu.be/uGEjO3-7EHA and https://youtu.be/KM-JdQCZ2Gw

How to Scan Your Chakras

1. Lie down, or have a friend help.
2. Hold your pendulum a few inches above the first chakra (base of the spine).
3. Ask: *"Is this chakra open and balanced?"*
4. Watch the movement. A steady circle often means balance, while no movement or a wobble may suggest blocked energy.
5. Move upward, checking each chakra one by one.

Pro Tip: Take notes in a journal. Over time, you'll notice patterns (like your throat chakra acting up before big presentations).

Important: A pendulum scan isn't a medical diagnosis. It's an energy check-in, like reading your emotional weather forecast. Always use it alongside common sense and self-care.

WANT TO SEE IT IN ACTION?

Reading is one thing—but sometimes you need to *see* this in real life. I've made a short video where I walk you through the steps, show you what the sways look like, and give you extra tips for getting clear results.

Watch it here: https://youtu.be/QcQTXV1dEJQ

Chakra Balancing with a Pendulum

Your pendulum isn't just for yes/no—it can actually help balance the energy centers of the body (called **chakras**). Think of it like a gentle energy broom that sweeps away stuck vibes.

What You'll Need

- A pendulum (necklace, charm, even a Christmas ornament on a string—anything that swings).
- A friend or partner who's comfortable lying down.
- A quiet space and (optional) a blanket to keep them cozy.

Step-by-Step Exercise

1. **Prepare the Space**
   o Have your friend lie down, arms at their sides.
   o Take a few deep breaths together to relax.

2. **Start the Scan**
   - Choose a chakra to begin with (you can start at the feet or crown—it doesn't matter, just stay consistent).
3. **Hold the Pendulum**
   - Position it a few inches above the chakra area. Don't touch the body.
   - Silently say: *"Pendulum, move in any direction needed to clear this chakra."*
4. **Wait and Watch**
   - Allow the pendulum to swing. It might circle, wobble, or swing side to side.
   - Be patient—sometimes it's quick, sometimes it takes a while.
   - If it feels like it's going forever, gently ask your friend to take a deep breath and wiggle their toes—this often resets the flow.
5. **Move Through the Chakras**
   - Repeat the process for each chakra: Root, Sacral, Solar Plexus, Heart, Throat, Third Eye, Crown.
   - You may switch hands if your arm gets tired.
6. **Closing the Session**
   - Once all chakras are cleared, take one final deep breath together.
   - Silently give thanks for the process and the healing.

Pro Tip: Keep notes in a journal after each session. Did one chakra take longer to clear? Did your friend feel lighter, calmer, or more energized afterward? Tracking experiences helps you see patterns.

Reminder: This is for energy balancing and relaxation—it's not a replacement for medical care.

WANT TO SEE IT IN ACTION?

Reading is one thing—but sometimes you need to *see* this in real life. I've made a short video where I walk you through the steps, show you what the sways look like, and give you extra tips for getting clear results.

Watch it here:

Check a Plant, Pet, or Crystal's Energy

Your pendulum isn't just for people—it can tune into the energy of anything alive or vibrating (and spoiler: *everything* vibrates).

Plants

1. Hold your pendulum a few inches above the leaves of a plant.
2. Ask: *"How is this plant's energy today?"*
3. A strong swing might mean it's thriving. A weak or sluggish swing may mean it needs water, sunlight, or love.

Fun idea: Try comparing a freshly watered plant vs. one you forgot about for a week. Notice the difference.

Pets

1. Sit near your dog, cat, or even hamster.
2. Hover the pendulum over their back or heart area.
3. Ask: *"Is [pet's name] feeling balanced and healthy?"*
4. The pendulum might swing strongly if all is well, or wobble/slow down if your pet is stressed.

Note: This is an **energy check**, not a vet visit. Always use real medical care when needed.

Crystals

1. Place your crystal on the table.
2. Hold your pendulum over it and ask: *"Is this crystal energetically clear?"*
3. If you get a sluggish or "no" response, give the crystal a cleanse (sunlight, moonlight, salt, or sound).
4. Re-test and see how the swing changes.

Try comparing a crystal you've used often with one you just bought—you'll likely notice the energy feels different.

Pro Tip: The pendulum doesn't just give a yes/no here—it can also show *strength*. A strong swing = strong energy. A weak swing = low or blocked energy.

The Vibration Counting Method

Everything carries a vibration—foods, objects, even people. Some things lift your energy; others drag it down. You can use your pendulum not just for yes/no, but to measure the *strength* of those vibrations.

Step 1: Teach Your Pendulum the Count

1. Hold your pendulum and manually move it **back and forth** to program it.
   - A full swing forward + back = **1 count.**
   - Only count on the *forward swing.* (So: 1, 2, 3, etc.)
2. Keep counting upward: 1–20, then by tens (30, 40, 50…), then hundreds, thousands, and even millions if you want to test high vibrations.
3. To end a test, move the pendulum on purpose:
   - **Clockwise circle = positive vibration.**
   - **Counterclockwise circle = negative vibration.**

Step 2: Test an Object

1. Place an item in front of you (try a pen, a piece of fruit, or even candy).
2. Hold the pendulum above the object.
3. Start counting while the pendulum swings forward.
4. When the pendulum reaches the "right number," it will shift into a circle.

Step 3: Read the Results

- **Clockwise circle = positive vibration.** The object is raising your energy.
- **Counterclockwise circle = negative vibration.** The object lowers your energy (common with junk food, processed items, or objects that carry heavy emotional vibes).

Example:

- You test a pen → pendulum circles at **200** → neutral/low vibration.
- You test fresh fruit → pendulum circles at **5,000** clockwise → high positive vibration.
- You test candy → pendulum circles at **300** counterclockwise → low/negative vibration.

WANT TO SEE IT IN ACTION?

Reading is one thing—but sometimes you need to *see* this in real life. I've made a short video where I walk you through the steps, show you what the sways look like, and give you extra tips for getting clear results.

Watch it here: https://youtu.be/0YQKMvc6JeA

STORY TIME: THE SALAD

When I first learned how to use a pendulum, I was excited to try it on everything—food, crystals, even random objects around the house. One evening, I was at a friend's house for dinner. She and her husband had made a beautiful salad, and she looked at me with a grin and said:

"Why don't you count the vibration of your salad?"

So, I pulled out my pendulum and began the test. Back and forth it swung as I counted—100, 200, 300… Then suddenly, the pendulum went absolutely wild. It spun and swirled like it had a mind of its own. I froze, shocked, and looked up at her.

"What just happened?" I asked.

She laughed and said, *"I blessed your salad."*

In that moment, I learned something powerful: our thoughts and intentions can instantly raise the vibration of anything—even a bowl of lettuce. The pendulum wasn't just reacting to the food, it was reacting to the love and blessing poured into it.

Lesson: Energy isn't only in objects—it's in the meaning we give them. A simple blessing, a kind thought, or gratitude before eating can raise the vibration of your food, your space, and even your day.

Quick Mood Test: *"What's My Vibe Right Now?"*

Sometimes you don't even know what mood you're in until it hits you later. Your pendulum can give you a sneak peek into your current vibe—like a mini emotional weather report.

Step 1: Get Centered

- Hold your pendulum steady in front of you.
- Take one deep breath in…and out.

Step 2: Ask the Question

- Say: *"What's my vibe right now?"*
- Watch the movement:
    - **Clockwise circle = positive/energized.**
    - **Counterclockwise circle = negative/drained.**

- o **Small or shaky swing = unclear, maybe you
  need rest or grounding.**
- o **Strong forward/back or side/side = a clear
  yes/no to a specific feeling (try pairing with
  questions below).**

Step 3: Get Specific

Follow up with more focused questions, like:

- *"Am I stressed?"*
- *"Am I excited?"*
- *"Do I need to recharge?"*
- *"Am I ready to be social?"*

Why This Works:
Your body and subconscious pick up on your real mood before
your conscious mind does. The pendulum makes those hidden
vibes visible, so you can decide what you actually need—
whether it's a nap, a snack, a walk, or a party.

MOOD SCALE GAME: RATE YOUR VIBE

Want to know not just *what* your mood is, but *how strong* it
feels? Try this mood scale test. It's like a pendulum-powered
"mood meter."

Step 1: Draw Your Scale

- On a piece of paper, write the numbers **1 through 10** in
  a row (or a circle if you like visuals).
- 1 = lowest energy/drained.
- 10 = highest energy/happy/charged up.

Step 2: Ask the Question

- Hold your pendulum above the scale.

- Ask: *"Where is my mood right now, from 1 to 10?"*

Step 3: Watch the Swing

- The pendulum will usually start to move toward one number.
- That's your current vibe rating.

Step 4: Check It Again Later

- Do the test in the morning, then again at night.
- Notice how your number changes depending on your day, your food, or even the people you've been around.

Fun Twist: Try the mood scale with friends before hanging out. Compare vibes and see if your pendulums "agree."

Note: A low number doesn't mean you're broken—it just means you might need a recharge (food, water, rest, or fun).

MOOD BOOST CHALLENGE

Your mood isn't stuck. You can shift your vibe in just a few minutes—and your pendulum can prove it.

Step 1: Test Your Starting Point

- Use the **Mood Scale Game** (1–10) to find your current vibe.
- Write down your number.

Step 2: Do a Quick Boost

Pick one of these simple mood lifters (or make your own):

- Blast your favorite song and dance like nobody's watching.

- Step outside for fresh air and sunlight.
- Chug a glass of water.
- Do three big stretches and a silly shake-out.
- Write down three things you're grateful for.
- Hug a pet, pillow, or person (consensually!).

Step 3: Retest Your Mood

- Hold the pendulum over your Mood Scale again.
- Ask: *"Where's my vibe now, from 1 to 10?"*
- Notice if the number went up.

Pro Tip: This works even better if you keep a journal. Over time, you'll discover your personal "mood hacks"—the fastest ways to raise your vibration when you need it most.

Pendulum & People (Friendship, Crushes, Decisions)

Pendulums aren't just for energy scans or food choices—they can also help you navigate the trickiest part of life: **relationships.** From best friends to crushes to big decisions, your pendulum can give you a peek at how your heart really feels.

Friendship Vibes

- Hold your pendulum and ask:
  "Is hanging out with [friend's name] today going to lift my energy?"
- Try testing before making plans—you might notice the pendulum says "no" on days when you'd be better off resting.

Tip: It's not about judging your friends, it's about checking whether *today* is the right vibe for you.

Crush Check (Just for Fun)

- Ask: *"Does thinking about [crush's name] raise my vibration?"*
- Watch how your pendulum swings.
- A "yes" swing might mean excitement, while a "no" swing could mean stress.

Important: Don't use the pendulum to spy or predict what someone else feels. It's a mirror of *your energy,* not their secret diary.

Decision Time

Friend drama? Too many invites? Or just can't decide what to do on Saturday night? Try **Pendulum Decision Roulette:**

1. Write your choices on slips of paper (Go to the party / Stay in / Hang out with bestie).
2. Place them in a circle.
3. Hold the pendulum in the center and ask: *"Which choice is best for me today?"*
4. Let it swing toward the winner.

Why This Works:
Your pendulum reflects your subconscious truth—the part of you that already knows what (or who) feels good for your energy.

Chapter 9: Talking to... Yourself (and Maybe More)

Higher Self, Intuition, Guides—Who's Really Answering?

Okay, so here's the big question: when your pendulum moves, *who's actually talking?* Is it your muscles, your subconscious, your higher self, your spirit guides, or maybe even something else?

The answer: it depends on who you ask.

1. The Science Answer: *It's You*

Scientists will say your brain is sending tiny signals (the ideomotor effect) based on what you already know deep down. In other words, it's your subconscious nudging your hand.

2. The Intuition Answer: *It's Still You, but Deeper*

Many people believe the pendulum taps into your **higher self**—the wise part of you that sees the bigger picture and isn't distracted by stress, fear, or ego. When you use a pendulum, you're bypassing the noise to hear your inner truth.

3. The Spiritual Answer: *You're Not Alone*

Others believe pendulums can connect you to **guides, angels, ancestors, or universal energy.** In this view, the pendulum is like a phone—you're holding the receiver, but the message might be coming from a team that's got your back.

Try This: Who's Answering?

1. Hold your pendulum and ask: *"Am I talking to my subconscious mind?"*
2. Ask: *"Am I talking to my higher self?"*
3. Ask: *"Am I talking to a guide or helper?"*
   Notice the swings. Your answers may surprise you—and they may change depending on the day or the question.

Important Note: Whoever you believe is answering, the pendulum works best when you set the intention. Before starting, try saying:
"I ask for answers that are clear, honest, and for my highest good."

That way, whether it's your own inner wisdom or something bigger, you're tuning into guidance you can trust.

Guardrails: Safe vs. Off-Limits Questions

Pendulums are powerful tools—but like any tool, they work best when used wisely. Some questions are totally safe and helpful. Others? Not so much. Here's your guide.

Safe Questions (Go For It!)

- Personal check-ins: *"Do I need more rest today?"*
- Healthier choices: *"Is water better for me right now than soda?"*

- Energy balance: *"Is my heart chakra open?"*
- Everyday decisions: *"Which homework should I do first?"*
- Friendship vibes: *"Will hanging out with [friend's name] boost my energy?"*

Off-Limits Questions (Don't Go There)

- Predicting someone else's thoughts/feelings: *"Does my crush like me back?"*
- Life-or-death health questions: *"Do I have [serious illness]?"*
- Fatalistic questions: *"Am I doomed to fail this test?"*
- Timing demands: *"Exactly what day will I get married?"*
- Messy what-ifs: *"Will my best friend betray me?"*

Why These Are Off-Limits:

Pendulums reflect *your* subconscious—not other people's private thoughts or the entire future. Asking loaded, scary, or vague questions usually gives confusing answers and creates anxiety instead of clarity.

Pro Tip: Ask Like a Scientist

If a question feels heavy or complicated, break it down into smaller yes/no pieces. Instead of *"Will I ever find love?"* try:

- *"Am I ready for a relationship right now?"*
- *"Is it in my best interest to meet new people this month?"*

The clearer the question, the clearer the answer.

Pendulum Prayer and Quiet Reflection

Your pendulum works best when you bring a clear, calm energy to it. Think of it like tuning an instrument—before you play, you set the tone. A simple prayer or moment of reflection helps align your mind, body, and spirit so your answers feel honest and steady.

A Simple Pendulum Prayer

Before you begin, hold your pendulum in your hand and say (out loud or silently):

"I ask for guidance that is clear, honest, and for my highest good. May my pendulum reflect truth, free from fear, bias, or distraction."

This short prayer reminds you that the pendulum is a tool for connection, not control.

Quiet Reflection Exercise

1. Sit comfortably with your pendulum in your hands.
2. Close your eyes and take three slow breaths.
3. Imagine a soft light surrounding you and your pendulum.
4. In your mind, say: *"I am centered. I am open. I am ready."*
5. When you feel calm, begin your practice.

Why It Helps:
This isn't about being religious—it's about creating a moment of stillness. When your energy is focused, your pendulum's answers are clearer.

Using a Pendulum for Hypnosis

When most people think of hypnosis, they picture someone swinging a pocket watch back and forth, whispering, *"You are getting sleepy..."* That image is actually based on the pendulum. While hypnosis today uses many techniques, the pendulum remains a powerful way to help the mind focus and relax.

Why It Works

- **Rhythm + Repetition:** The steady, predictable swing gives the brain a single point of focus, which quiets distractions.
- **The Trance Effect:** Watching the pendulum can shift the brain into a relaxed, suggestible state (similar to daydreaming).
- **Self-Hypnosis:** You don't always need a hypnotist— watching your own pendulum can help you reach a meditative, calm, or focused state.

Step-by-Step: Self-Hypnosis with a Pendulum

1. **Set Up**
   - Sit in a comfortable chair.
   - Hold the pendulum at eye level so it dangles and swings easily.
2. **Focus**
   - Begin swinging the pendulum gently side to side.
   - Fix your gaze on the motion. Don't force your eyes—just follow naturally.
3. **Breathe & Relax**
   - With each swing, take slow, steady breaths.
   - Think: *"With each swing, I feel more calm."*
4. **Suggestion Phase**
   - Once you feel deeply relaxed, add gentle affirmations:
     - *"My mind is calm and clear."*
     - *"I feel safe and focused."*
     - *"My body knows how to release stress."*
5. **Return**
   - When ready, count upward from 1 to 5, imagining yourself becoming more awake and energized.
   - Stop the pendulum and stretch lightly.

Variations

- **Guided Hypnosis:** Have a partner swing the pendulum while speaking affirmations.
- **Focus Aid:** Use the pendulum to focus before studying, creating, or meditating.
- **Stress Release:** Ask the pendulum to "swing away" tension as you watch it.

Pro Tip: Hypnosis isn't about control—it's about focus. You're always in charge. The pendulum simply gives your mind a rhythm to follow so relaxation feels effortless.

Chapter 10: Skeptics, Science & Secret Powers

What Scientists Say (and Why They're Partly Right)

Not everyone believes in pendulums. In fact, some scientists roll their eyes and say it's "just your muscles moving." But here's the thing: they're not totally wrong.

The Science Side

Researchers often explain pendulums with something called the **ideomotor effect**—tiny, unconscious muscle movements your brain makes without you realizing.

- When you *think* "swing forward," your hand actually makes micro-movements that push the pendulum that way.
- You don't notice it, but the pendulum shows it loud and clear.
- Same thing happens in Ouija boards and lie detector tests.

So yes, part of pendulum magic really is **you moving it without knowing.**

But Here's the Catch

If it's "just" your muscles—then *who's controlling the muscles?*

- Your subconscious?
- Your intuition?
- Your higher self?

Even scientists admit the subconscious brain is a powerhouse, processing way more than your conscious mind ever could. It picks up on clues, patterns, and energy signals your "thinking brain" misses. The pendulum makes those hidden insights visible.

Why They're Only Partly Right

Science explains **how** the pendulum moves—but not always **why it gives useful answers.**

- Why do some people get the same results over and over, even with blind tests?
- Why do pendulums sometimes reveal things you didn't consciously know yet?
- Why do blessings (like the salad story!) or intentions raise the "vibration" results?

That's where the mystery comes in—and why pendulums live in the space between **science and secret powers.**

The Fun Part: You don't have to pick a side. You can believe in the ideomotor effect *and* still explore energy, intuition, and vibes. In fact, blending both makes pendulum practice even more exciting.

Placebo as Proof: Intention Matters

Here's something wild: scientists love to dismiss pendulums as "just a placebo." But what if the placebo effect isn't proof that pendulums don't work—but proof that they *do*?

What's Placebo?

In science experiments, the **placebo effect** is when someone feels better just because they *believe* they're getting medicine—even if it's just a sugar pill. Their body actually responds to their expectation.

How This Connects to Pendulums

When you hold a pendulum with the intention of getting guidance, your belief focuses your energy. That focus creates tiny muscle movements (the ideomotor effect) and, more importantly, opens your subconscious to answers.

So in a way, pendulums *are* a placebo—but that doesn't mean they're fake. It means your **belief and intention are the real engine.**

Why That's Powerful

- If intention alone can make people heal, relax, or feel energized, then intention is a superpower.
- Pendulums give your intention a visible form—swinging yes, no, or maybe.
- The more you believe in the process, the clearer the answers become.

Lesson: Don't be embarrassed if skeptics say, *"It's just a placebo."* Say thank you. A placebo is proof that your mind is powerful enough to change reality with belief.

MIND OVER MATTER TEST

If intention really matters, you should be able to *see* it with your pendulum. Try this experiment and watch how your thoughts change the swing.

Step 1: Pick Your Test Object

- A glass of water works best.
- You can also try food, a crystal, or even a favorite object.

Step 2: Test the Starting Vibration

- Hold your pendulum above the object.
- Ask: *"Show me the vibration of this [water/food/object]."*
- Start counting (1–20, then 30, 40, 50, etc.) until the pendulum shifts into a circle.
- Note the number and whether the circle is clockwise (positive) or counterclockwise (negative).

Step 3: Add Intention

- Place your hands around the object (or just focus on it).
- Say: *"I bless this [water/food/object] with love and light."*
- Visualize it glowing brighter.
- Do this for about 30–60 seconds.

Step 4: Retest

- Hold your pendulum above the object again.
- Repeat the vibration count.
- Notice if the number is higher or the swing stronger than before.

What You'll Learn: Intention shifts energy. If your pendulum shows a stronger or higher vibration after you focus on blessing the object, that's proof that your belief and focus have real power.

Why Belief Isn't Fake—It's Fuel

A lot of skeptics say, *"That's not real—it's just in your head."* But here's the twist: that's exactly why it works.

Belief = Activation

When you believe something is possible, your brain and body line up to make it happen.

- Athletes use visualization before games, and their muscles fire as if they're already moving.
- Placebo studies prove that belief alone can lower pain, speed up healing, and change body chemistry.
- In pendulum work, belief focuses your micro-movements and tunes your subconscious into clarity.

Fake vs. Fuel

- **Fake** means nothing's happening.
- **Fuel** means your belief is the spark that makes everything else run.

Belief doesn't make pendulum answers imaginary—it makes them **visible.** Your faith in the process unlocks your subconscious, connects you to your intuition, and maybe even opens a line to something bigger.

Lesson: Don't let anyone tell you belief is "just pretending." It's the battery that powers your pendulum.

DARE TO BELIEVE CHALLENGE

Want proof that belief is the real fuel? Try this two-step test.

Step 1: Test With Doubt

1. Hold your pendulum steady.
2. Ask a simple, true question (like: *"Is my name [your name]?"*).
3. But this time, silently think: *"This won't work. Nothing is happening. This is fake."*
4. Watch the swing—it may feel weak, shaky, or hesitant.

Step 2: Test With Belief

1. Reset your pendulum to stillness.
2. Ask the same question again.
3. This time, silently think: *"This works. I trust my pendulum. My energy is strong."*
4. Watch the swing—notice how much clearer and stronger it feels.

Step 3: Compare

Write down what you noticed in both rounds. Most people see a huge difference—the "belief round" makes the pendulum swing bigger, faster, and with more confidence.

Takeaway: Belief isn't decoration. It's the difference between a flicker and a flame. Your pendulum runs on the energy you feed it.

Chapter 11: Pendulum Games

Truth or Dare: Pendulum Edition

Why should pendulums only be used for serious stuff? They make awesome party games, too. One of the most fun ways to play is a twist on the classic: **Truth or Dare—Pendulum Style.**

How to Play

1. **Get Your Group Ready:** Grab a few friends and a pendulum (or have each person use their own).
2. **Set the Rules:** Keep dares safe and silly (no mean stuff).
3. **Take Turns:** When it's your turn, ask the pendulum:
   o *"Truth or dare?"*
   o Watch the swing: one direction = truth, the other = dare. (Decide this together before you start.)

Truth Round

If the pendulum picks truth, the group gets to ask you a yes/no question.

- Example: *"Do you secretly like pineapple on pizza?"*
- Use the pendulum to answer.

Dare Round

If the pendulum picks dare, the pendulum decides what you do.

- Example: Write a list of dares on slips of paper, put them in a bowl, and ask:
  "Pendulum, should I do this one?" until it says yes.
- Or let the pendulum pick from numbered dares.

Fun Twist: You can also let the pendulum decide who goes next by writing everyone's name on paper slips in a circle and asking, *"Who's up?"*

Safety Reminder: Keep the game lighthearted. The pendulum is for fun here, not embarrassing secrets or dangerous dares.

Blindfold Guessing Game

Think you and your pendulum are really in sync? Put it to the test with this energy-based guessing game.

How to Play (Solo Version)

1. **Set Up the Mystery:** Gather 3–5 small objects (a coin, a crystal, a key, a piece of candy, etc.). Place them in separate cups or boxes.
2. **Blindfold Yourself:** Shuffle the containers (or ask a friend to) so you don't know which is which.
3. **Ask the Pendulum:** Hover over each container and ask:
   o *"Is the crystal in here?"*
   o *"Is the candy in this one?"*
4. **Reveal the Answer:** Lift the lid and see if your pendulum was right.

Group Version

1. One person hides the object while the others are blindfolded.
2. Each player takes turns using their pendulum to figure out which container holds the item.
3. Keep score to see who's the best energy detective.

Pro Tip: Start with just one object (like a coin hidden under one of three cups). As you get better, make it harder by adding more items or asking specific yes/no questions about what's inside.

Reminder: This isn't about "psychic perfection." It's a playful way to practice trusting your pendulum.

The Pendulum Race: Who Swings First?

Want to turn pendulum practice into a full-on competition? Try the **Pendulum Race.** It's fast, funny, and shows who can get their pendulum swinging on command the quickest.

How to Play

1. **Gather Players:** Everyone grabs their pendulum and sits at the same table (or in a circle).
2. **Pick the Motion:** Decide the target swing— forward/back, side/side, or a circle.
3. **Start Line:** Hold pendulums perfectly still above the table.
4. **Go!** Someone shouts, "Ready, set, swing!"
5. **Race:** Each player asks their pendulum to move in the chosen direction.
6. **Winner:** The first pendulum to clearly swing in that direction gets the point.

Variations

- **Relay Race:** After the first motion, the group switches directions (circle, then side-to-side). Whoever completes all motions fastest wins.
- **Team Race:** Split into two teams. First pendulum on each team races, then the next player goes, passing the "energy baton."
- **Slow & Steady:** Instead of fastest, race to see whose pendulum makes the *biggest swing* in 30 seconds.

Pro Tip: This game is less about speed and more about **focus + belief.** The calmer and clearer your intention, the faster your pendulum responds.

Mystery Box

Setup:

- Place 3–5 small objects (rock, snack, coin, key, crystal, etc.) inside separate opaque boxes, bags, or cups.
- Only one person knows what's inside.

How to Play:

1. Each player takes turns holding their pendulum over a box.
2. Ask yes/no questions to narrow it down:
   - *"Is there food in this box?"*
   - *"Is it metal?"*
   - *"Is it something I could wear?"*
3. After 3–5 questions, they make their final guess.
4. Reveal the object!

Why it's fun: It's like 20 Questions but with a pendulum twist.

Guess the Object

Setup:

- A partner picks one item from a group of 5–10 options. Place all items in front of the players.

How to Play:

1. Hold the pendulum over each object, asking: *"Is this the chosen object?"*
2. The pendulum gives yes/no responses until the right item is found.
3. Swap roles so everyone gets a turn hiding and guessing.

Why it's fun: You get immediate feedback—right or wrong—so it builds trust in your pendulum quickly.

Future Forecast

Setup:

- Each player writes a simple yes/no future question on a slip of paper (examples: *"Will it rain tomorrow?" "Will we have a pop quiz this week?" "Will my team win on Saturday?"*).

How to Play:

1. Use the pendulum to answer each question in turn.
2. Record all the answers in a journal or group scoreboard.
3. At the end of the week, check which predictions came true.

Why it's fun: It feels like fortune-telling, but it's really a long-term accuracy test—and it gets more exciting as results play out.

Treasure Hunt Challenge

Turn pendulum practice into a game with friends or family:

1. **Hide the Treasure**
   - One person hides a small object (coin, crystal, key, candy) somewhere in the room.
   - Make sure it's hidden but not impossible (no duct taping things under floorboards, please).
2. **Draw the Map**
   - Sketch a quick floor plan of the room or area.
   - Mark off different zones (bed, desk, couch, kitchen table).
3. **Pendulum Detectives**
   - Each player uses their pendulum to hover over the map and ask:
     "Is the treasure in this zone?"
   - Once they get a "yes," they head to that area to search physically.
4. **Race to Find It**
   - Whoever finds the hidden object first wins!
   - Swap roles and play again.

Fun Twist: Keep score or award silly prizes—like letting the winner pick the next snack, movie, or TikTok challenge.

30-Day Challenge: Track Your Accuracy

Want to know if your pendulum skills are really getting sharper? Put yourself to the test with a **30-day accuracy challenge.** This isn't about being perfect—it's about building trust in your connection and watching your progress grow.

Step 1: Set Up Your Journal

Create a page (or use a notebook) with columns like this:

| Date | Question Asked | Pendulum Answer | Real Outcome | Accurate? | Notes |

Step 2: Ask Everyday Questions

Each day, test your pendulum on 1–3 **checkable** questions. Examples:

- *"Will I get a text from [friend's name] today?"*
- *"Will it rain today?"* (check the forecast later)
- *"Will I finish my homework before 9 pm?"*
- *"Is this snack going to make me feel good?"* (note how you feel after)

Step 3: Record the Outcome

At the end of the day, write down what actually happened. Did your pendulum call it right?

Step 4: Look for Patterns

At the end of 30 days:

- Count your total "accurate" vs. "inaccurate" answers.
- Notice which types of questions gave the clearest results (health, food, school, relationships).
- See if your accuracy improved as the days went on.

 Pro Tip: Don't sweat mistakes. In fact, inaccuracies teach you where wording or emotions may have influenced your results. That's part of the growth.

Charts, Graphs & Pendulum Tools

Beyond Yes/No — Unlocking More Information

A pendulum isn't limited to swinging yes or no. With charts and graphs, you can expand your questions and get more detailed answers. Think of it as going from a "light switch" to a "whole control panel."

Why Use Charts?

- They give more nuanced answers (percentages, multiple options).
- They make practice more visual and interactive.
- They help you "measure" things like energy levels, emotions, or priorities.

Types of Charts You Can Make

1. **Yes/No/Maybe Wheel**
   - Draw a circle divided into three parts. Label them *Yes, No, Maybe*.

- o Hold your pendulum in the center—let it swing toward the answer.
2. **Percentage Scale**
   - o Draw a line marked 0% to 100%.
   - o Ask: *"How aligned am I with this choice?"*
   - o Watch where the pendulum points.
3. **Alphabet Chart**
   - o Write out A–Z in a half-circle.
   - o Use this to "spell out" words (great for practicing subconscious writing).
4. **Emotion Wheel**
   - o Create a circle with slices labeled (Happy, Stressed, Calm, Excited, Tired, Angry, etc.).
   - o Ask: *"What's my current dominant emotion?"*
   - o Let the pendulum swing to your mood.
5. **Decision Graph**
   - o Make a chart with different options (Outfit A, Outfit B, Outfit C; or Job 1, Job 2, Job 3).
   - o Place your pendulum in the center and ask: *"Which choice is best right now?"*

How to Make Your Own

1. Grab paper and a pen (or print templates if you like).
2. Decide what you want to measure (mood, food, study choices, etc.).
3. Draw a circle, line, or wheel.
4. Label each section clearly.
5. Hold your pendulum at the center or start point.

Try This: Chart Practice

1. Make a **Yes/No/Maybe Wheel.**
2. Ask silly questions first: *"Is pizza a vegetable?"* *"Am I secretly a superhero?"*
3. Then try a real one: *"Is Outfit A better for today than Outfit B?"*

4. Notice how the pendulum swings toward each labeled section.

Pro Tip: Charts are like training wheels. The more you use them, the stronger your pendulum connection gets—even when you go back to simple yes/no.

Note: Keep your questions **clear and specific.** A vague chart just confuses your pendulum.

WANT TO SEE IT IN ACTION?

Reading is one thing—but sometimes you need to *see* this in real life. I've made a short video where I walk you through the steps, show you what the sways look like, and give you extra tips for getting clear results.

Watch it here: https://youtu.be/M4TIautOQT8

Charts

Using the Pendulum Rating Scale

This chart works like a measuring stick for your pendulum. Instead of only yes/no, you can now check intensity, strength, or accuracy on a scale.

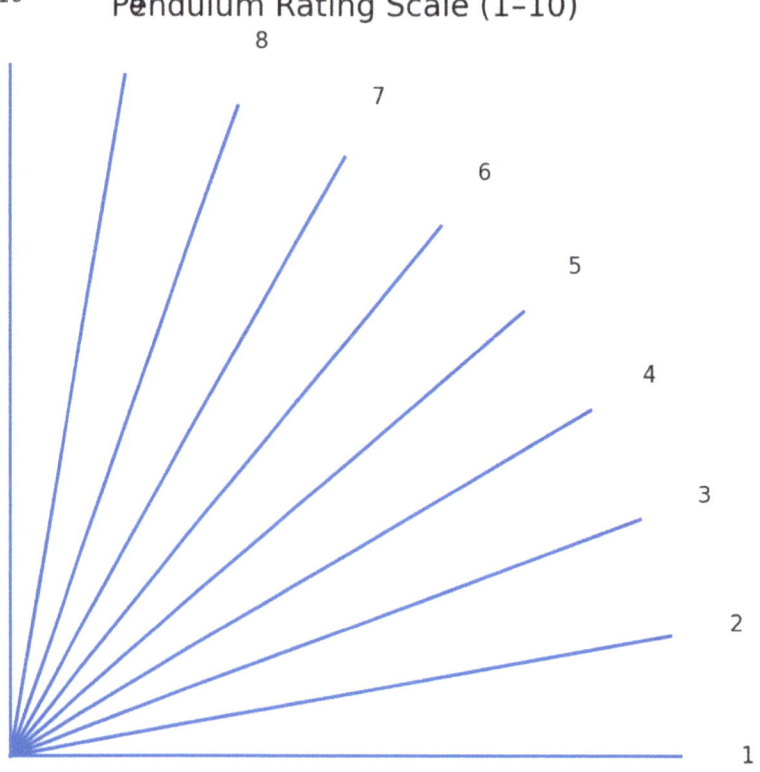

Pendulum Rating Scale (1–10)

Step-by-Step

1. **Set Your Question**
   - Example: *"On a scale of 1–10, how energized will this food make me?"*
   - Keep it clear and specific.
2. **Hold Steady**
   - Place your pendulum at the center point of the fan (where all the lines meet).
   - Keep your elbow supported so only the pendulum moves.
3. **Ask & Wait**
   - Ask your question once.
   - Watch which line (number) the pendulum swings toward.
4. **Read the Number**
   - If it swings between two lines (say, 6 and 7), your answer is "in between."
   - If it circles instead of pointing, it may mean "ask a clearer question."
5. **Confirm**
   - If unsure, ask again in a different way.
   - Example: *"Is the answer higher than 5?"* (Yes/No). Narrow it down.

Changing the Numbers

- Want a 1–5 scale instead? Just relabel: 1, 2, 3, 4, 5.
- Want 0–100? Redraw the fan with more ticks or use a printed 0–100 chart.
- Want really big numbers (1–1,000)? Use this chart to locate the "band" (low, medium, high), then switch to counting (forward-back = 1, 2, 3…) until the pendulum circles.

Pro Tip: These charts are flexible! Use them for:

- **Energy check** (How strong is my vibe today?)
- **Confidence check** (How confident am I about this decision?)
- **Compatibility check** (How good of a match is this option for me?)

Using the Pendulum Decision Wheel

This wheel gives you four simple answers: **Yes, No, Maybe, Ask a Better Question.**
It's perfect when you want more nuance than just yes/no.

Pendulum Decision Wheel

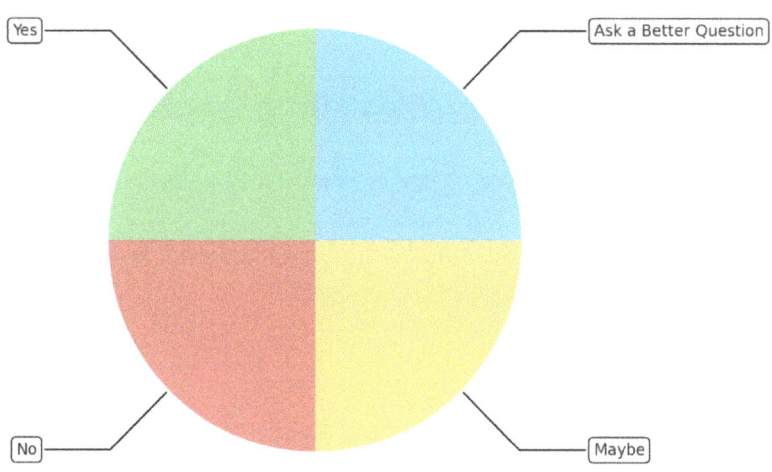

Step-by-Step

1. **Set Your Intention**
   o Place your pendulum over the center of the wheel.
   o Think clearly about your question. Example: *"Is this the best time to start my project?"*
2. **Hold Steady**

- o Rest your elbow on a table so your arm doesn't wobble.
- o Keep the pendulum directly above the center circle.

3. **Ask the Question**
   - o Ask once, silently or aloud.
   - o Wait for the pendulum to swing.

4. **Watch the Direction**
   - o The pendulum will begin to swing toward one of the quadrants.
   - o Read the answer where the swing points: Yes, No, Maybe, or Ask a Better Question.

5. **Refine if Needed**
   - o If you get "Maybe," it usually means part of the answer isn't clear yet.
   - o If you get "Ask a Better Question," rephrase your question so it's simpler or more specific.

Changing the Wheel

- Want only Yes/No? Redraw the wheel with two halves.
- Want more nuance? Add sections like *Not Now, Try Again Tomorrow, and Needs Clarification.*
- You can even make themed wheels (example: *Which chakra needs support?* or *Which food group does my body need right now?*).

Pro Tip: The "Ask a Better Question" section is the most powerful—because it reminds you that the pendulum can only answer what you ask. The clearer the question, the clearer the answer.

Using the Pendulum Decision Chart

Sometimes life doesn't give you a simple yes or no—it gives you options. This chart helps your pendulum swing toward the choice most aligned with you right now.

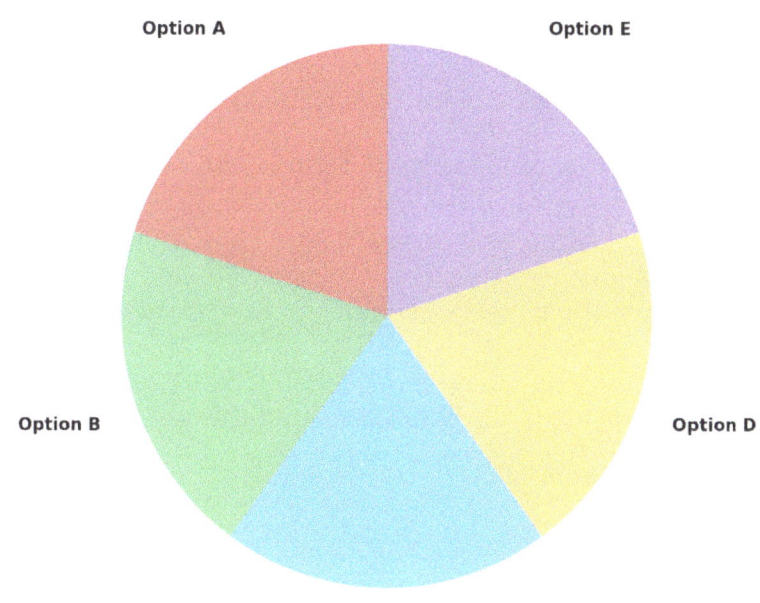

Pendulum Decision Chart

Option A · Option E · Option B · Option D · Option C

Step-by-Step

1. **List Your Options**
   - Label the chart sections with the choices you're deciding between.
   - Example: *Option A = College, Option B = Job, Option C = Gap Year, Option D = Travel, Option E = Business.*

2. **Set Your Intention**
   - ○ Hold the pendulum over the center of the chart.
   - ○ Say (silently or aloud): *"Which option is in my highest alignment right now?"*

3. **Hold Steady**
   - ○ Rest your elbow on a table to keep your arm still.
   - ○ Keep the pendulum hanging directly over the center.

4. **Ask the Question**
   - ○ Ask clearly and once. Don't reword mid-swing.
   - ○ Example: *"Which of these options is best for me today?"*

5. **Watch the Swing**
   - ○ The pendulum will begin to move in the direction of one of the labeled slices.
   - ○ That's your strongest match.

6. **Double-Check**
   - ○ If it points between two slices, ask follow-up questions:
     - ▪ *"Is it more Option B than Option C?"*
   - ○ If the pendulum stalls or circles, it could mean: *"Ask a better or more specific question."*

Variations

- **Daily Decisions:** Snacks, outfits, activities.
- **Big Life Choices:** Careers, moves, relationships.
- **Fun Group Play:** Everyone adds one option to the chart (movies, restaurants, vacation spots) and sees what the pendulum picks.

Pro Tip: Decision charts don't predict the future—they reflect your subconscious alignment in the present. If your priorities change, so will the pendulum's answer.

Using the Chakra Pendulum Wheel

This wheel helps you identify which of your chakras needs attention, clearing, or balancing. Each slice corresponds to one of the seven major chakras.

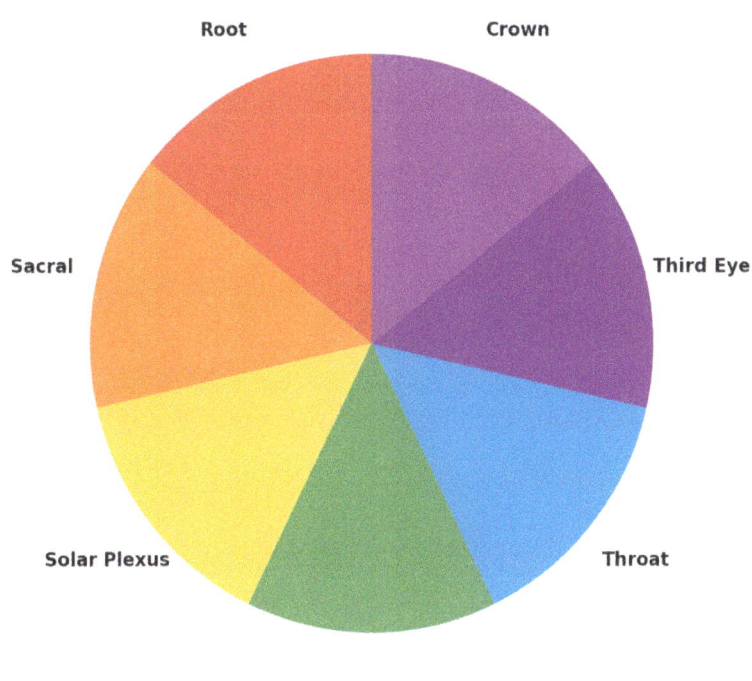

Chakra Pendulum Wheel

Step-by-Step

1. **Prepare Your Space**
   - Sit comfortably with your pendulum.
   - Take a few deep breaths to ground and center yourself.
2. **Set Your Intention**
   - Place the pendulum over the center of the wheel.

     o Say (silently or aloud): *"Which chakra needs my focus right now?"*

3. **Hold Steady**
   - o Keep your elbow supported so only the pendulum moves.
   - o Relax your hand—don't try to force the swing.

4. **Ask the Question**
   - o Examples:
     - ▪ *"Which chakra is most out of balance?"*
     - ▪ *"Which chakra needs clearing today?"*
     - ▪ *"Where should I focus my meditation?"*

5. **Read the Answer**
   - o Watch which slice the pendulum swings toward.
   - o That chakra is the one needing attention.

6. **Follow Up**
   - o Once identified, you can:
     - ▪ Meditate on that chakra's color.
     - ▪ Place a crystal over that chakra.
     - ▪ Use the **Chakra Balancing Exercise** (from earlier in your book).

Variations

- **Partner Scan:** Have a friend lie down, hold your pendulum over the wheel, and ask: *"Which chakra in their body needs balancing right now?"*
- **Daily Check-In:** Use the wheel each morning to see which chakra could use extra support during the day.
- **Affirmation Support:** Ask: *"Which chakra needs a positive affirmation today?"*

Pro Tip: If the pendulum points equally between two chakras, it often means they're connected. For example, Heart + Throat could signal that expressing emotions needs balance.

Using the Aura Pendulum Wheel

Your aura is said to be the energy field that surrounds your body. Its colors can shift with your mood, health, and spiritual state. This wheel helps you identify the dominant vibration in your aura right now.

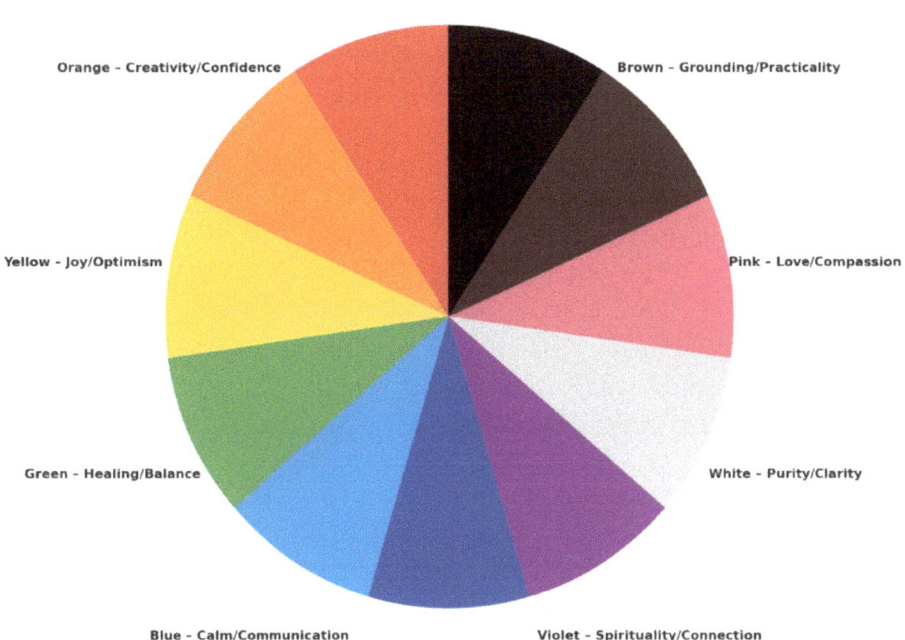

Step-by-Step

1. **Prepare Yourself**
   o Sit comfortably and relax your shoulders.
   o Take a few deep breaths, imagining your energy field expanding gently around you.
2. **Set Your Intention**
   o Hold your pendulum over the center of the Aura Wheel.
   o Ask: *"What color is strongest in my aura right now?"*
   o Or: *"Which aura quality most influences me today?"*
3. **Hold Steady**
   o Keep your elbow supported so your arm doesn't shake.
   o Let the pendulum move naturally—don't force the swing.
4. **Read the Answer**
   o The pendulum will swing toward a color section.
   o Each color has a meaning (e.g., Green = Healing/Balance, Pink = Love/Compassion, Indigo = Intuition/Insight).
5. **Interpret the Message**
   o Use the meaning of the chosen color to reflect on your energy.
   o Example: A swing toward Yellow (Joy/Optimism) could mean you're radiating positivity, or that you need more joy in your life.
6. **Follow Up**
   o Ask clarifying questions, like:
      ▪ *"Is this color dominant in my physical, emotional, or spiritual layer?"*
      ▪ *"Is this aura color helping or draining me?"*

Variations

- **Daily Aura Check:** Use the wheel each morning to see what energy you're starting with.
- **Before/After:** Check your aura color before meditation, then again afterward, and compare.
- **Other People/Objects:** With permission, hover your pendulum near someone else, or over a crystal, plant, or even a room, and ask which aura color dominates.

Pro Tip: Aura readings aren't about perfection—they're about reflection. Let the colors be invitations to notice your inner state.

Using the Pendulum Emotion Wheel

This wheel lets your pendulum point to your dominant emotion (or the emotion you most need to acknowledge) in the moment.

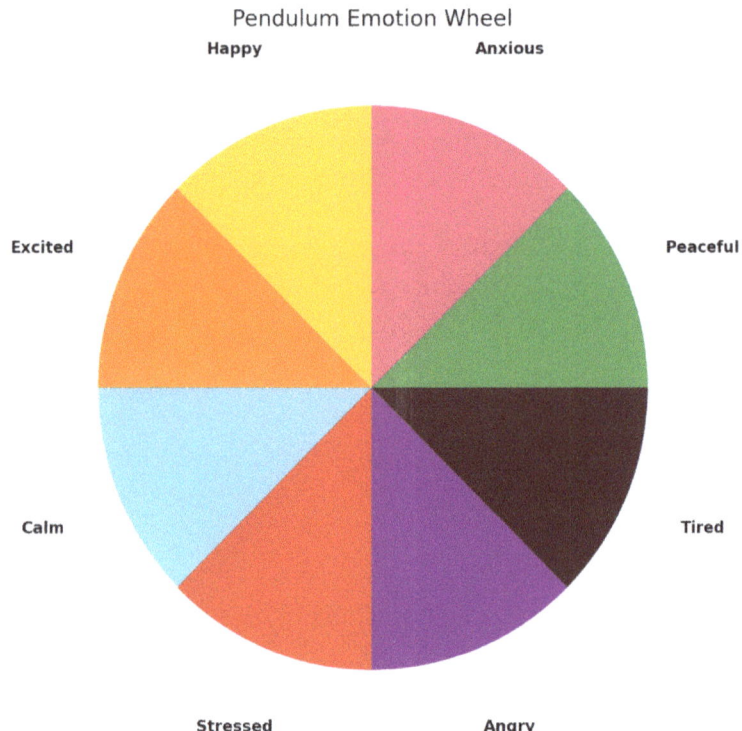

Pendulum Emotion Wheel

Step-by-Step

1. **Center Yourself**
   - Take a deep breath, relax your shoulders, and clear your mind.
2. **Set Your Intention**
   - Hold the pendulum over the center of the wheel.
   - Ask: *"Which emotion am I feeling most right now?"*

- o Or: *"Which emotion is affecting me the most today?"*
3. **Watch the Swing**
   - o The pendulum will swing toward one of the labeled emotions.
   - o That's the energy you may be carrying in this moment.
4. **Reflect**
   - o Don't judge the answer. Instead, ask yourself: *"Where is this showing up in my life? What can I do with it?"*
5. **Optional Follow-Up**
   - o Ask: *"What's the healthiest action I can take with this emotion?"*
   - o Or use the **Decision Chart** to see possible responses.

Other Emotions You Can Add

If you want more nuance, redraw or expand your wheel with some of these:

- **Positive / Uplifting:** Joyful, Loving, Grateful, Inspired, Hopeful, Proud, Playful
- **Neutral / Subtle:** Curious, Thoughtful, Distracted, Sensitive, Restless
- **Challenging / Heavy:** Lonely, Overwhelmed, Guilty, Resentful, Fearful, Confused, Hopeless

Pro Tip: You can create a **tiered Emotion Wheel** (like the "Plutchik's Wheel of Emotions" used in psychology) with primary emotions in the center (Joy, Anger, Fear, Sadness, Surprise, Disgust) and more specific ones radiating outward.

Using the Human Body Pendulum Chart

This chart helps you check which part of the body—or which body system—needs attention, balance, or energy clearing. It's not a medical diagnostic tool, but it can help identify areas that warrant attention, care, or professional follow-up.

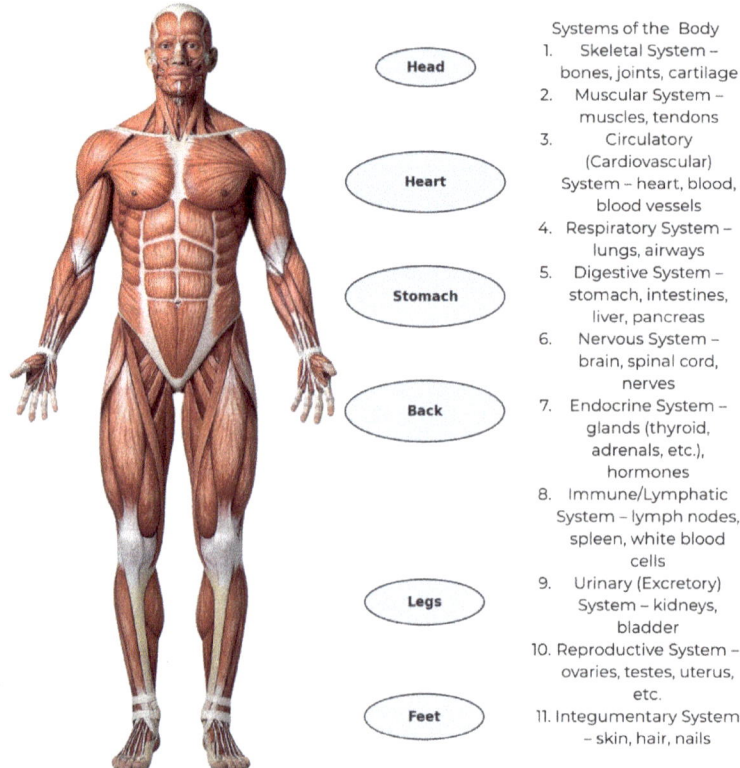

Systems of the Body

1. Skeletal System – bones, joints, cartilage
2. Muscular System – muscles, tendons
3. Circulatory (Cardiovascular) System – heart, blood, blood vessels
4. Respiratory System – lungs, airways
5. Digestive System – stomach, intestines, liver, pancreas
6. Nervous System – brain, spinal cord, nerves
7. Endocrine System – glands (thyroid, adrenals, etc.), hormones
8. Immune/Lymphatic System – lymph nodes, spleen, white blood cells
9. Urinary (Excretory) System – kidneys, bladder
10. Reproductive System – ovaries, testes, uterus, etc.
11. Integumentary System – skin, hair, nails

Step-by-Step

1. **Prepare Your Space**
   - Place the chart in front of you on a table.
   - Hold your pendulum above the center of the body outline.
   - Take a few grounding breaths.

2. **Set Your Intention**
   - ○ Say: *"Show me where my energy is most imbalanced right now."*
   - ○ Or: *"Which system of my body needs support today?"*
3. **Hover & Watch**
   - ○ Let the pendulum swing.
   - ○ Notice if it points toward one of the labeled areas (Head, Heart, Stomach, Back, Legs, Feet).
4. **Cross-Reference with Systems**
   - ○ Once an area is highlighted, check the list of **systems of the body** connected to that region.
   - ○ Example: If it points to the *Stomach*, you may want to reflect on the **Digestive System** (stomach, intestines, liver, pancreas).
5. **Ask Clarifying Questions**
   - ○ "Is this imbalance physical, emotional, or energetic?"
   - ○ "Is it connected to diet, stress, or rest?"
   - ○ "Would this benefit from movement, water, or stillness?"
6. **Respond with Care**
   - ○ Use the information as guidance for self-care (meditation, nutrition, rest, gentle movement).
   - ○ Always seek medical help for serious concerns— this chart is for *insight*, not replacement of healthcare.

Variations

- **Daily Energy Scan:** Use the chart each morning to see where your body may need extra support.
- **Before/After Comparison:** Try before meditation, exercise, or healing work, then compare results after.
- **Partner Practice:** With permission, hold the pendulum over the chart while focusing on another person to see what area needs balancing.

Pro Tip: Sometimes the pendulum will point to multiple areas. Write them down and look for connections (e.g., Back + Heart could suggest posture and stress are linked).

Using the Pendulum When/Date Chart

This chart is for timing questions. Instead of asking only *if* something will happen, you can check *when*.

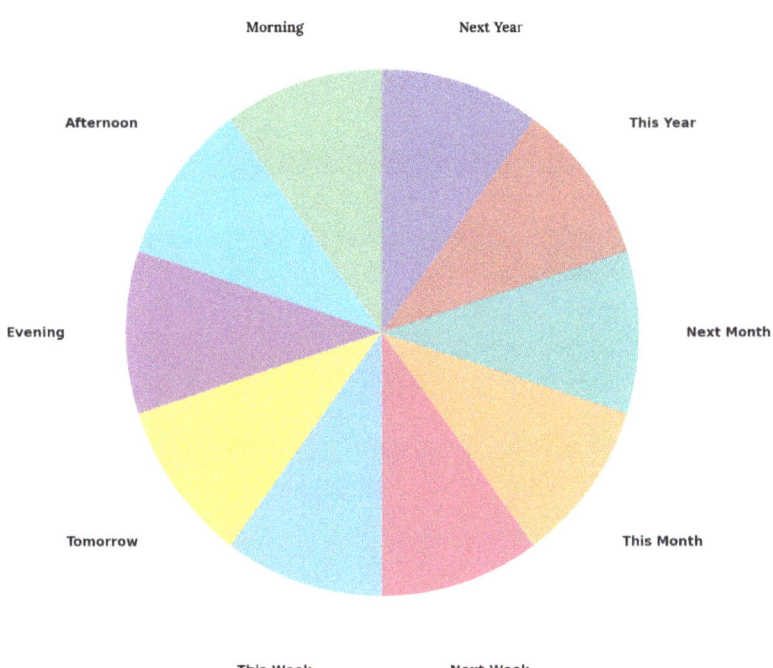

Step-by-Step

1. **Phrase the Question Clearly**
   o Example:
       ▪ *"When is the best time to start my project?"*
       ▪ *"When will I receive clarity on this situation?"*
2. **Hold Over the Center**

- o Place the pendulum directly over the middle of the chart.
- o Rest your elbow so only the pendulum moves.

3. **Ask Once, Wait**
   - o Ask your question aloud or silently.
   - o Let the pendulum swing naturally toward one of the timeframes.

4. **Read the Section**
   - o If it swings toward *Morning, Afternoon, or Evening* → the answer is soon (today or tomorrow).
   - o If it swings toward *This Week, Next Week, This Month* → short-term timing.
   - o If it swings toward *Next Month, This Year, Next Year* → medium to long-term timing.

5. **Confirm if Needed**
   - o If it swings between two slices, ask follow-ups:
     - ▪ *"Is it this week?"*
     - ▪ *"Is it next week?"*

Variations

- **Personal Timing:** "When is the best time for me to [meditate/exercise/study]?"
- **Event Timing:** "When will the right opportunity arrive?"
- **Daily Use:** "When today should I focus on this task?"

Pro Tip: Timing with a pendulum is very literal. If you get "Tomorrow," it means *the soonest energy is aligned then,* not always a guarantee. Use timing charts as guidance, not set-in-stone predictions.

Using the Food, Supplements & Vitamins Wheel

Your body is constantly sending signals about what it needs.
This chart helps you tune in and check which category of food
or nutrient is most supportive for you right now.

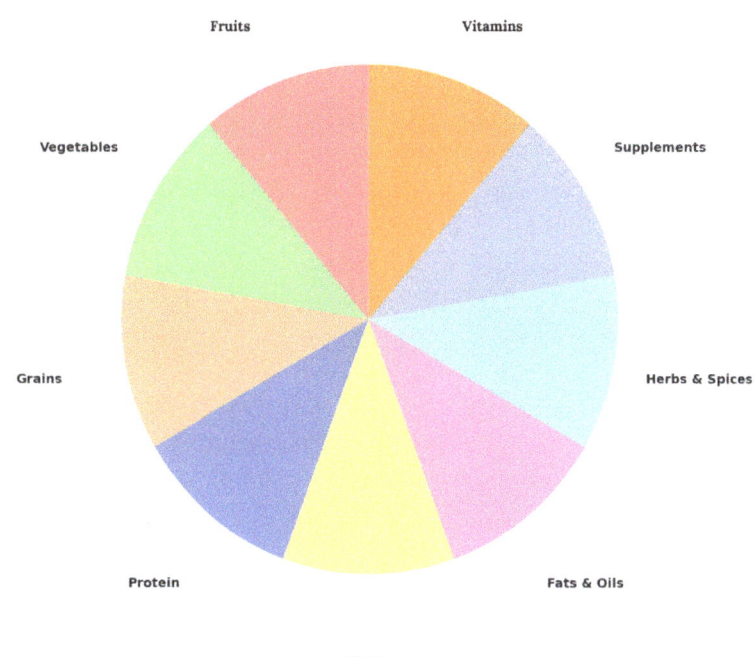

Step-by-Step

1. **Set Your Intention**
   - Hold your pendulum over the center of the
     wheel.
   - Ask: *"What does my body need most right
     now?"*

- o Or: *"Which food/supplement group will best support my energy today?"*

2. **Hold Steady**
   - o Keep your elbow on the table and let the pendulum swing freely.
   - o Don't try to control the motion—let it guide itself.

3. **Read the Result**
   - o The pendulum will swing toward one of the categories:
     - ▪ **Fruits, Vegetables, Grains, Protein, Dairy, Fats & Oils, Herbs & Spices, Supplements, Vitamins**

4. **Refine if Needed**
   - o If the pendulum points to "Supplements," ask follow-ups:
     - ▪ *"Which type—minerals, probiotics, omega-3, or herbs?"*
   - o If it points to "Vitamins," follow with:
     - ▪ *"Which vitamin—C, D, B-complex, etc.?"*

5. **Apply with Awareness**
   - o Use results as a *guide,* not as medical advice.
   - o If your pendulum keeps pointing to the same group (e.g., Vegetables or Water-rich foods), notice the pattern and reflect on your habits.

Variations

- **Meal Planning:** Ask before preparing meals: *"Which food group will balance me best today?"*
- **Daily Health Check:** Do a quick check-in each morning for your body's top need.
- **Seasonal Balance:** Ask weekly which group supports you most for the current season.

Pro Tip: Always phrase your question for **the present moment.** Instead of *"What do I need in general?"* ask *"What does my body need most right now, today?"*

Pendulum Allergies Chart

Your body is constantly giving you clues about what feels supportive and what doesn't. Sometimes those signals show up as energy dips, skin reactions, or digestive discomfort. This chart helps you tune in with your pendulum to explore which category of allergens may be affecting you most right now.

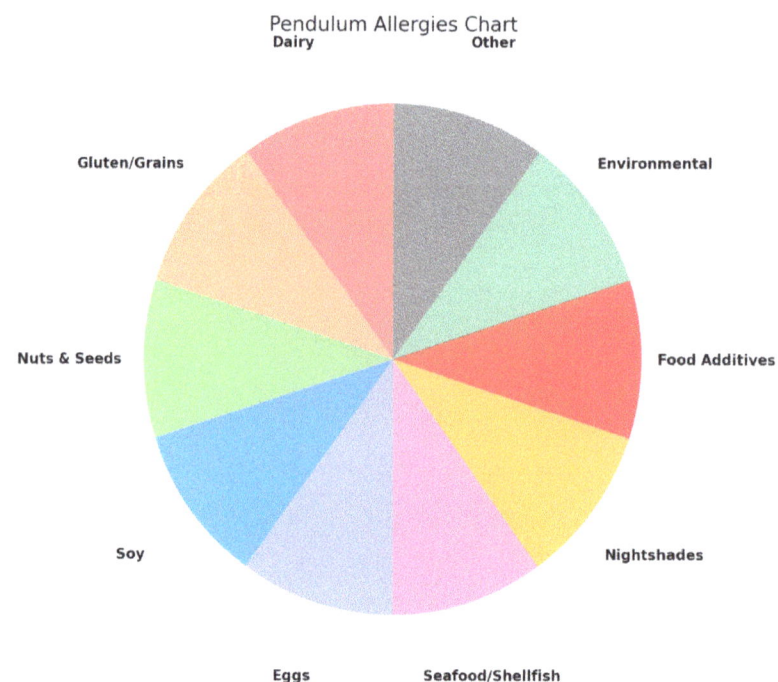

Pendulum Allergies Chart

Step-by-Step

1. **Ask Broad First**
   - Hold the pendulum over the wheel.
   - Ask: *"Which category of allergen is most affecting me right now?"*

2. **Narrow It Down**
   - If the pendulum points to *Dairy*, for example, ask:
     - *"Is it milk? Cheese? Yogurt?"*
   - For *Environmental*, ask:
     - *"Is it dust? Pollen? Mold? Pets?"*
3. **Confirm with Yes/No**
   - Use your Yes/No signals to double-check once you've narrowed to a specific trigger.
4. **Track Results**
   - Keep a journal of answers. Over time, patterns may emerge.

Important Note: This chart is for *self-awareness and energy insight only*. It's not a substitute for medical allergy testing. Always consult a healthcare professional for actual diagnoses or severe reactions.

Categories for the Wheel:

- **Dairy** 🥛 (milk, cheese, yogurt)
- **Gluten/Grains** 🌾 (wheat, barley, rye)
- **Nuts & Seeds** 🥜 (peanuts, almonds, sesame)
- **Soy** 🌱
- **Eggs** ⚪
- **Seafood/Shellfish** 🐟
- **Nightshades** 🍅 (tomatoes, peppers, eggplant, potatoes)
- **Food Additives** 🧬 (MSG, dyes, preservatives)
- **Environmental** 🌿 (pollen, dust, mold, pet dander)
- **Other** ❓ (catch-all category for unusual or uncommon triggers)

Variations

- **Daily Check-In:** Each morning, ask: *"Is my body reacting to any allergen category today?"*
- **Food Testing:** Before eating, ask: *"Would this food trigger sensitivity for me right now?"*
- **Environment Scan:** Use the chart to check if your energy is reacting to things like dust, pollen, or pets.
- **Seasonal Shifts:** Ask weekly: *"Which allergen category is most affecting me this season?"*

Pro Tip

Always frame your question for the **present moment.** Instead of asking, *"Am I allergic to this?"* (too absolute), ask: *"Is my body reacting to this right now?"*

Questions to Ask...*or Not*

Top 10 Pendulum Questions Teens Actually Want to Ask

1. *"Will texting [name] right now make things better or just awkward?"* 💬 😬
2. *"Is this outfit giving main character energy today?"* 👗 ✨
3. *"Will coffee help me survive first period, or just make me jittery?"* ☕ 🥱
4. *"Is this friend actually mad at me, or am I overthinking again?"* 🧠 🔄
5. *"Will taking a nap help, or will I wake up more tired?"* 😴 ⚡
6. *"Is it smarter to study now or binge Netflix and regret it later?"* 📚 🍿
7. *"Does my playlist match my vibe today?"* 🎶 🌈
8. *"Should I say yes to this invite, or will it be awkward central?"* 🎉 😐
9. *"Will eating this leftover pizza give me life or regret?"* 🍕 🤢
10. *"Is it worth risking it to post this on TikTok?"* 📱 🔥

Why These Work

Because they're the questions you actually wonder about day-to-day. They're still **specific, in the moment, and about YOU**—but they don't sound boring or textbook-y.

Pro Tip: If you ever ask something and your pendulum acts "weird" (circles, stalls, swings tiny), it's probably saying: *"Dude, rephrase that."*

Top 10 Funny (But Useless) Pendulum Questions

1. *"Do my fries love me back?"* 🍟 ❤️
2. *"Will I be TikTok famous tomorrow?"* 📱 ✨
3. *"Is pizza secretly a vegetable?"* 🍕 🥦
4. *"Will my dog learn to talk if I ask nicely?"* 🐶 🗣️
5. *"Am I going to Hogwarts next year?"* 🧙 🦉
6. *"Does my phone miss me when I'm asleep?"* 📱 💤
7. *"Will my crush dump their crush for me by Friday?"* 💔 ➡️ 💖
8. *"Is my math homework evil?"* ➕ ➖ 😈
9. *"Can I time-travel if I believe hard enough?"* ⏳ 🚀
10. *"Will my pendulum ever swing me into outer space?"* 🔮 🪐

Why These Don't Work

Because your pendulum isn't a comedian, psychic hotline, or genie. It works best when you ask **clear, literal, and realistic questions.** If your question sounds like a meme, you'll probably just get circles or nonsense.

Pro Tip: Laugh at the silly questions—but then practice turning them into *useful* ones.
Example: Instead of *"Does my crush like me?"* ask:
➡️ *"Is it in my best interest to spend time with [crush's name] this week?"*

Pendulum for Career & College Choices

Snacks and playlists are fun—but pendulums can also help with the *big* stuff, like what to do after high school, what career paths to explore, or even which college to choose.

The trick? Remember that the pendulum doesn't "predict" your future. It shows you what aligns best with your energy *right now*. Think of it as a way to cut through confusion and hear what your subconscious already knows.

Step-by-Step: Using Your Pendulum for Big Decisions

1. **Get Specific**
   - Instead of: *"Should I go to college?"*
   - Ask: *"Would going to [specific college] this year support my growth?"*
   - Or: *"Is studying [career path] aligned with me right now?"*
2. **Use the Decision Chart**
   - Write options around a decision wheel (College A, College B, Gap Year, Job, Trade School).
   - Hold your pendulum in the middle and ask:
     - *"Which option is in my best interest right now?"*
3. **Check the Timing**
   - Sometimes the answer isn't "no"—it's "not yet."
   - Use your **When/Date Chart**:
     - *"Is this the right year to start this path?"*
4. **Double-Check With % Scales**
   - Use your **0–100 chart**:
     - *"What percent aligned am I with [Option A]?"*
     - Compare scores across different choices.
5. **Follow With Real-World Action**
   - The pendulum helps with clarity, but research, visits, and talking to mentors seal the deal.

- o Use pendulum insights as a compass, not the whole map.

Example Questions

- *"Would I thrive more in a small college or a large university?"*
- *"Which subject area (arts, science, business, trades) is most aligned with me right now?"*
- *"Is taking a gap year a good choice for me this year?"*
- *"Will studying in [city or country] support my growth?"*
- *"Is this scholarship worth applying for?"*

Pro Tip: Careers evolve. Don't stress about finding your *forever* path. Use the pendulum to check alignment with your *next best step.*

Pendulum Life Hacks

Pendulum for Stress & Anxiety Relief

Stress is like an invisible backpack—sometimes you don't even realize how heavy it's gotten until you stop and check. Your pendulum can be a quick tool to measure it and even help release it.

Step 1: Check Your Stress Level

1. Hold your pendulum over a **1–10 rating chart**.
2. Ask: *"Show me how much stress I'm holding right now."*
3. Notice where it swings. That's your starting point.

Step 2: Breathe It Out

1. Take slow, deep breaths—in through your nose, out through your mouth.
2. Imagine stress leaving your body with every exhale.
3. After a minute, ask again: *"What's my stress level now?"*
4. Keep breathing until the number drops.

Step 3: Pendulum Breathing Game

1. Gently swing your pendulum forward and back.
2. **Inhale** as it swings forward, **exhale** as it swings back.
3. Let the rhythm guide you for 10–20 swings.
4. Notice how calm your body feels afterward.

Pro Tip: This isn't about getting the number down to zero. It's about noticing, breathing, and letting your body reset. Even dropping from an 8 to a 6 is progress.

Pendulum & Friendships

Friends can be your biggest cheerleaders… or sometimes your biggest stress. The pendulum can help you check in with your energy around different relationships—without judgment.

Friendship Questions to Ask with Your Pendulum

- *"Is this friendship supportive of me right now?"*
- *"Is it in my best interest to spend time with [name] today?"*
- *"Does spending time with [name] help me feel more like myself?"*
- *"Is this friend a positive influence on me right now?"*
- *"Will saying yes to hanging out with [friend/group] be good for my energy today?"*
- *"Is this the right time to talk to [friend's name] about what's on my mind?"*
- *"Is this friendship helping me grow in a good way right now?"*
- *"Would it be better for me to take a break from this friendship today?"*
- *"Is this friend being honest with me right now?"*
- *"Do I feel safe being myself in this friendship?"*

Pro Tip: Phrase friendship questions like you're checking a vibe *today.* Keep them short, specific, and personal. The pendulum reflects *your feelings in the moment,* not a forever prediction.

Friendship Game: Circle of Truth

1. Gather a group of friends and sit in a circle.
2. Place a pendulum in the center.
3. Each person takes turns asking a fun question, like:
   - *"Am I the funniest one here?"*
   - *"Does someone in this circle have a secret crush?"*
   - *"Will we all still be friends next year?"*
4. The pendulum swings, everyone laughs, and you learn how playful this tool can be.

Tip: Keep it light! This is about bonding, not roasting.

Pro Tip: Friendship questions work best in the **present moment.** Instead of asking, *"Will we be best friends forever?"* (that's too big), ask, *"Is this friendship good for me right now?"*

Pendulum & Digital Life

Let's be real: so much of life happens online—scrolling, posting, snapping, streaming. Sometimes it's fun. Sometimes it's draining. Your pendulum can help you figure out the difference before you get sucked in too deep.

Questions to Ask Before You Post

- "Will posting this make me feel proud tomorrow?"
- "Is this post something I won't regret later?"
- "Does this photo/text/video reflect the real me?"
- "Will sharing this attract positive attention?"
- "Is this post respectful of myself and others?"
- "Will I still be okay with this post a month from now?"
- "Is this the right time to post this?"
- "Would keeping this private be better for me?"
- "Is this post aligned with how I want to be seen?"
- "Will this post make me feel lighter, not heavier?"

Pro Tip: If you're not sure about posting, that's already your intuition whispering. The pendulum just makes the whisper louder.

SCREEN TIME CHECK

- *"Do I need more rest than scrolling right now?"*
- *"Would putting my phone down be better for my mood today?"*
- *"Will another hour online leave me feeling drained?"*

Try this as a quick vibe check before you dive into a binge.

THE SOCIAL MEDIA DETOX CHALLENGE

1. Hold your pendulum and ask:
   - *"How many hours of screen time would be healthiest for me today?"* (use the 1–10 chart).
2. Write that number down.
3. Challenge yourself to stick to it—and check again tomorrow.

You can even make it a game with friends: everyone asks their pendulum, sets a limit, and compares at the end of the day.

Pro Tip: Your pendulum won't tell you to delete TikTok or throw away your phone—it just helps you notice when your energy is asking for something different.

Pendulum & Creativity

Ever feel stuck on what to draw, write, or create? Your pendulum can be like a randomizer for inspiration. Instead of staring at a blank page, you give yourself options, then let the pendulum pick.

Step 1: Make a Creativity Chart

1. Grab a piece of paper.
2. Draw a big circle (like a pie).
3. Divide it into slices—anywhere from 4 to 12 works great.
4. Label each slice with creative options. For example:
   - **Colors:** Red, Blue, Green, Yellow, Purple, Black, White, Gold, Silver.
   - **Ideas:** Character, Poem, Song lyric, Abstract doodle, Short story, Comic panel.
   - **Mediums:** Paint, Markers, Collage, Digital, Pencil sketch.

Pro Tip: Keep it playful. The more random the options, the more fun the results.

Step 2: Ask Your Question

- *"What color should I paint with today?"* (point to your Color Wheel).
- *"Which idea should I try next in my project?"* (use your Ideas Chart).
- *"What medium should I use for this piece?"* (use your Mediums Chart).

Step 3: Pendulum Poetry

1. Create a **Word Wheel** with random words (funny, dramatic, abstract, or totally weird).
2. Hold the pendulum in the center.
3. Ask: *"Which word should I use first?"*
4. Write it down. Repeat until you've got a short poem or lyric.
   - Example words: Sky, Flame, Lost, Echo, Pizza, Thunder, Glow, Dream.

Pro Tip: Don't take it too seriously. This is about sparking ideas, not making a masterpiece. Sometimes the "wrong" color or random word is what pushes you into a new creative flow.

Pendulum Journaling Prompts

Journaling doesn't have to be "dear diary, today I felt…" boring. Think of it like a creative challenge. Your pendulum picks the topic, you get to make it fun.

Quick & Fun Prompt Chart

Make a wheel or list with light, playful categories:

- The funniest thing that happened this week
- A secret dream (wild or serious)
- If I had a superpower, it would be…
- My top 5 songs right now
- The best meal I ever ate
- A made-up story about my future self
- A person I'd want to swap lives with for a day
- The most random thought I had today

Ask: *"What should I write about today?"* Swing, pick, and go.

Creative Prompts

- *"What color matches my mood today?"* → Write about why.
- *"If today was a movie, what would the title be?"*
- *"What emoji describes me right now?"*

Fast-Write Challenge

Ask your pendulum: *"How many minutes should I write for?"* (use your number chart).

- 2 minutes? Go!
- 7 minutes? Challenge accepted.
- 10 minutes? That's practically a novel.

Pro Tip: Don't overthink it. The pendulum is just here to break the "blank page" freeze. Write like no one's grading you.

Pendulum & Better Grades

Nope, the pendulum won't whisper test answers in your ear. But it *can* help you study smarter, stay focused, and calm your nerves—three things that make grades a lot better.

Your pendulum doesn't replace hard work. But it's like a study buddy that helps you pick smarter battles, calm test nerves, and stop wasting time guessing what to focus on.

1. WHAT SHOULD I STUDY FIRST?

You sit down to do homework, and suddenly every subject feels like it's yelling at you. Math wants your brain. English wants an essay. Science wants notes reviewed. History wants dates memorized. Overwhelm = instant procrastination.

Your pendulum can help you stop spinning and just pick a starting point.

Step-by-Step

1. **Make a Study Chart**
   o Draw a circle and divide it into slices.

- o Label each slice with your subjects (Math, English, Science, History, Languages, etc.).
- o If you only have a couple of assignments, make each slice one task instead (Example: *Math worksheet, English essay outline, History reading*).

2. **Set the Intention**
   - o Hold the pendulum over the center of the chart.
   - o Ask: *"Which subject needs my focus most right now?"*
   - o Keep it simple, and ask only once.
3. **Read the Answer**
   - o The pendulum will swing toward one of the slices.
   - o That's your starting point—no debating, no second-guessing.
4. **Do the Work**
   - o Commit to at least 20–30 minutes of that subject.
   - o Once it's done (or you've made solid progress), go back to the chart and ask again: *"Which subject is next?"*

The Cheat Code

- **Cuts Decision Fatigue:** Instead of wasting 20 minutes deciding what to do, you start right away.
- **Prioritizes Naturally:** Sometimes your brain knows what's urgent even when you don't admit it. The pendulum brings that to the surface.
- **Breaks Procrastination:** You don't have to choose— you just *do what the pendulum says.*

Pro Tip for Teens: If the pendulum keeps pointing to the same subject, it might mean that's the one stressing you out most. Do it first and get it off your back—you'll feel way lighter for the rest of your study session.

2. STUDY STYLE CHECK

Everyone learns differently. Some people remember better by *writing things down,* others by *speaking it out loud,* and some by *doing practice problems until it sticks.* The pendulum can help you figure out which style will actually work for you *right now.*

Step-by-Step

1. **Pick Your Options**
   o   Make a short list of possible study methods:
      ▪   Flashcards
      ▪   Rereading notes
      ▪   Highlighting
      ▪   Practice problems
      ▪   Teaching the material to a friend (or yourself out loud)
      ▪   Watching a video tutorial
2. **Ask One at a Time**
   o   Hold your pendulum steady.
   o   Ask: *"Will flashcards help me more than rereading notes right now?"*
   o   Then: *"Would practice problems be better than highlighting right now?"*
   o   Work through your options with yes/no questions.
3. **Pick the Winner**
   o   The pendulum will point you toward the style your subconscious feels will stick best.
   o   Go with that method for your study session.

The Cheat Code

- **Saves Time:** No more wasting an hour highlighting when what you really needed was practice problems.

- **Custom to You:** What works for one subject (like flashcards in Spanish) might not work for another (like math). The pendulum helps you match the right tool to the right subject.
- **Boosts Confidence:** Once you commit to a style, you stop second-guessing and just dive in.

Pro Tip for Teens: Don't assume one method always works. Before each subject, ask your pendulum which style to use. Sometimes your brain wants something new to stay engaged.

3. TIMING YOUR SESSIONS

Studying for hours straight doesn't always help—you end up zoning out, scrolling your phone, or memorizing nothing. On the flip side, if you study for too little time, nothing sticks. Your pendulum can help you find the *sweet spot* every time you sit down.

Step-by-Step

1. **Make a Number Chart**
   - Draw a circle divided into slices and label them with study session times: 10 min, 15 min, 20 min, 30 min, 45 min, 60 min.
   - Or just use your pendulum's yes/no with a written list.
2. **Ask the Question**
   - Hold the pendulum steady over the chart or list.
   - Ask: *"What's the best study session length for me right now?"*
3. **Do the Session**
   - Set a timer for whatever number the pendulum points to.
   - Focus on just that block of time. No distractions.
4. **Take a Break**

- o After your timer goes off, step away. Stretch, drink water, or scroll for a few minutes.
- o Then check with your pendulum again: *"How long should my next session be?"*

The Cheat Code

- **Stops Overload:** Your brain learns best in chunks, not marathons.
- **Adapts Daily:** Some days you're in the zone (45 minutes). Other days, you need shorter bursts (15 minutes). The pendulum adjusts to you.
- **Ends Procrastination:** You don't have to think, *"Should I study an hour or not at all?"*—the pendulum gives you a starting point.

Pro Tip: If your pendulum points to something tiny like 10 minutes, don't laugh—just do it. Starting small gets you moving, and momentum makes studying easier.

4. TEST STRESS RELIEF

Exams can turn your brain into static—heart racing, palms sweaty, thoughts all over the place. Your pendulum can help you measure your stress and actually bring it down before the test even starts.

Step-by-Step

1. **Check Your Stress Level**
   - o Hold your pendulum over a 1–10 number chart.
   - o Ask: *"What's my stress level right now?"*
   - o Notice where it swings (7? 9? Yep, that's your nervous system talking).
2. **Do Pendulum Breathing**
   - o Swing your pendulum forward and back.

- Inhale as it swings forward, exhale as it swings back.
- Imagine stress leaving with every exhale.
- Keep going for at least 10–20 swings.

3. **Recheck Your Stress**
   - Ask again: *"What's my stress level now?"*
   - Keep repeating until the number drops (even a 1–2 point drop makes a huge difference).

The Cheat Code

- **Instant Reset:** Instead of spiraling, you focus on rhythm + breath.
- **Brain Boost:** A calmer brain actually remembers more and processes faster.
- **Confidence Hack:** Knowing you can shift your stress gives you control before walking into the exam.

Pro Tip: Even if you don't have your pendulum during a test, you can *remember the swing* and breathe with that rhythm in your head. Your body will still calm down.

5. FOCUS QUESTIONS

Sometimes the hardest part of studying isn't the material—it's knowing what to *actually* focus on. Your pendulum can cut through the "I don't know where to start" fog and help you target what matters.

Questions to Ask

- *"Will studying this chapter help me more than that one?"*
  Use for choosing between topics when time is short.
- *"Do I already know this material well enough?"*
  If the pendulum says yes, move on. Don't waste time on what's already in your brain.

- *"Would a break right now improve my focus?"*
  Sometimes your brain is screaming for rest. A 5–10 minute reset can make the next session twice as productive.
- *"Is this the most important thing for me to review today?"*
  Helps you catch the real priority when you're juggling multiple subjects.
- *"Will practicing problems be more useful than rereading this chapter?"*
  Tailors your method to the material (math ≠ history ≠ English).

The Cheat Code

- **Targets Priorities:** No more wasting time on stuff you already know.
- **Boosts Efficiency:** A focused 20 minutes beats an unfocused 2 hours.
- **Builds Confidence:** Knowing you studied the right things lowers test anxiety.

Pro Tip: Write down the answers your pendulum gives. By test day, you'll know you've covered what matters most—and you'll feel way more ready.

Pendulum & Safety: Questions That Could Save Your Life

Life isn't just about grades and snacks—sometimes you face choices that feel big, scary, or risky. Your pendulum can help you pause, check in with yourself, and hear what your intuition is already screaming.

Questions to Ask Before Acting

- *"Is it in my best interest to go to this party tonight?"*
- *"Will going with this group of friends keep me safe right now?"*
- *"Is it safer for me to stay home tonight?"*
- *"Would leaving this place right now protect me?"*
- *"Is running away the best option for me right now?"*
- *"Will talking to an adult I trust help me in this situation?"*
- *"Is this person I'm with safe for me?"*
- *"Will taking this ride home be safe for me?"*
- *"Is it a good idea for me to drink/eat what's being offered?"*
- *"Will saying no here protect me?"*

The Cheat Code

- **Instant Pause Button:** Asking a pendulum slows you down before making a risky move.
- **Backs Up Your Gut:** Usually you *already know* the answer—the pendulum just makes it louder.
- **Keeps It About You:** These questions are about your safety, not predicting what other people will do.

Pro Tip: If your pendulum says *"no"* and your gut agrees, listen. But if you ever feel unsafe, don't stop at the pendulum—call a trusted friend, parent, or adult immediately.

Important: A pendulum is a tool, not a substitute for real-world safety. Always trust your instincts and get help if you feel in danger.

WHAT YOUR PARENTS WISHED YOU WOULD ASK (BUT PROBABLY WON'T)

Sure, your parents might bug you about homework, bedtimes, and making good choices. But here's the truth: if they could sneak questions into your pendulum sessions, these are the ones they'd probably want you to ask.

Safety Stuff

- *"Is going to this party a smart move for me right now?"*
- *"Will getting in that car be safe?"*
- *"Would staying home tonight keep me out of trouble?"*

Health Stuff

- *"Should I actually drink water instead of energy drinks right now?"*
- *"Will going to bed earlier help me feel better tomorrow?"*
- *"Is this junk food going to make me crash before practice?"*

School Stuff

- *"Is it smarter to finish my homework now instead of waiting until midnight?"*
- *"Would studying for 20 minutes help me more than scrolling TikTok for an hour?"*
- *"Will asking my teacher for help improve my grade?"*

Friendship Stuff

- *"Is this friendship good for me right now?"*
- *"Is it in my best interest to spend more time with people who lift me up?"*

- *"Would talking to my parents about this actually help?"*
(Spoiler: usually, yes.)

Honesty & Communication Stuff

Pendulum prompts that could actually improve parent-teen relationships:

- *"Would telling my parents how I feel about this help?"*
- *"Is it a good idea to ask for help instead of hiding this?"*
- *"Would being honest right now make things better in the long run?"*

Emotional Awareness Without Pressure Stuff

Parents want kids to notice their own feelings—without lectures. The pendulum can help.

- *"Am I stressed right now?"*
- *"Would journaling or talking to someone help me process this?"*
- *"Is my mood today more about me than about my friends?"*
- *Is my mood today hormonal?*

Pro Tip: You don't have to tell your parents you asked these questions. But if your pendulum gives you a "yes" and your gut agrees... maybe they were right all along.

Parent–Child Pendulum Trust Exercise

One of the coolest things about pendulums is how they can open up honest conversations. This exercise is designed for parents and teens to do *together*—building trust, practicing clarity, and learning to respect answers without judgment.

Step 1: Write the Question

- The teen writes down a clear, specific, yes/no/maybe question.
    - Example: *"Is it in my best interest to go to this party tonight?"*
    - Or: *"Will doing this activity support me right now?"*
- Parent can do the same with their own question if they like.

Step 2: Use the Pendulum

- The parent holds the pendulum over the paper and asks the teen's question out loud.
- The pendulum swings to "Yes," "No," "Maybe," or "Ask a Better Question."
- (Swap roles if you want: teen holds pendulum for parent's question.)

Step 3: The Agreement

- **Rule #1:** Both parent and teen agree in advance that whatever the pendulum says, the answer will be respected.
    - If it says "Yes" to going to a party → the parent agrees to trust it.
    - If it says "No" → the teen agrees to respect it.
    - "Maybe" or "Ask a Better Question" means: rewrite the question more clearly and ask again.

Why This Works

- **Builds Trust:** Both sides learn to respect the process and each other.
- **Removes Pressure:** Instead of arguing, the pendulum becomes the "neutral third voice."
- **Creates Honesty:** Writing questions down forces clarity. No vague half-asks.
- **Opens Conversation:** Afterward, parent and teen can talk about how they felt with the answer.

Pro Tip: Use this exercise for *important but not life-or-death* decisions first (like going to a party, joining a club, or trying out for a team). Once trust is built, you can use it for bigger choices.

REVERSE QUESTION WRITING FOR HONESTY

Sometimes, parents (or kids) already have an answer they *want* the pendulum to give. To keep things honest, you can flip the way the question is written—so no one can "nudge" the pendulum toward their preference.

How It Works

1. **Start With Intention**
   - Before asking, say out loud: *"I answer with honesty and integrity."*
   - This sets the ground rule: no trying to force the swing.
2. **Reverse the Wording**
   - Instead of asking only in the way that *you* want to hear... write it either way.
   - Example:
     - *"Is it in my best interest to go to the party tonight?"*
     - *"Is it in my best interest **not** to go to the party tonight?"*

- o   Ask both and see if the pendulum gives consistent, honest swings.

3. **Keep Each Side Simple**
    - o   Don't load the question with reasons (*"since I've been so good all week"*).
    - o   Just plain yes/no phrasing—one version forward, one reversed.

4. **Respect the Answer**
    - o   Parent and child both agree before starting: whatever comes up, it's valid.

Why This Matters

- **Keeps It Fair:** Stops anyone from "leaning" the pendulum with their hopes.
- **Builds Trust:** Both sides know the answer was neutral and double-checked.
- **Encourages Integrity:** Saying *"honesty and integrity"* before answering keeps everyone accountable.

Pro Tip: If you ask both the normal and the reverse version, and the pendulum gives the same clear answer each time, you know you've hit truth.

Conclusion: Stay Curious

Your pendulum may be a simple tool, but it opens the door to something extraordinary. Each swing is a dialogue between your body, mind, and spirit. Sometimes it feels like science. Sometimes it feels like magic. Most of the time—it's a little of both.

At first, the pendulum acts like training wheels for your intuition. You lean on it for guidance, letting it reveal what your inner voice already knows. Over time, though, you'll notice a shift. You won't always need the pendulum to confirm the answer—you'll begin to sense it directly. That's when you realize the pendulum was never the source of the wisdom. It was the mirror. The practice ground. The bridge to trusting yourself.

Science explains pendulums through the ideomotor effect—tiny, unconscious muscle movements. Spiritual traditions see them as a way to tune into energy, vibration, or guidance from beyond. The truth? Both perspectives hold value. The pendulum is powerful precisely because it lets you stand in both worlds at once: the logical and the mysterious, the measurable and the magical.

And here's the secret: you'll never "finish" learning with a pendulum. Each swing is another experiment. Today, it might help you choose a snack. Tomorrow, it could check your energy. Someday, it may help you pause before a big decision and find clarity in yourself that you didn't know was there.

In the end, the pendulum isn't really about yes or no. It's about staying curious—about asking better questions, playing with possibilities, and learning to trust the compass inside you.

So keep swinging, keep testing, keep exploring. The pendulum's greatest gift is not the answers it gives, but the confidence it awakens in you.

Bibliography

Science & Psychology of Pendulums

- Carpenter, William B. *On the Influence of Suggestion in Modifying and Directing Muscular Movement, Independently of Volition.* The Royal Institution of Great Britain, 1852. (Classic paper describing the ideomotor effect.)
- Hyman, Ray. *The Ideomotor Effect: A Review.* Journal of the Society for Psychical Research, 1999.
- Kirsch, Irving. *The Placebo Effect Revisited: Lessons Learned to Date.* Advances in Mind-Body Medicine, 2010.

Applied Kinesiology & Muscle Testing

- Goodheart, George J. *Applied Kinesiology.* S. Weiser, 1964. (Foundational text introducing applied kinesiology.)
- Walther, David S. *Applied Kinesiology: Synopsis.* Systems DC, 1988.
- Thie, John F. *Touch for Health: A Practical Guide to Natural Health with Acupressure Touch and Massage.* DeVorss & Company, 1973. (The classic guide for laypeople and practitioners.)
- Tuttle, Wayne. *Applied Kinesiology: Advanced Procedures and Techniques.* Tuttle Publishing, 2004.

BodyTalk & Energy Medicine

- Veltheim, John. *The BodyTalk System: Accessing the Body's Inner Compass.* PaRama, 2000.
- Veltheim, Esther & John. *MindScape: Access Your Inner Universe.* BodyTalk System Publishing, 2000.
- Eden, Donna. *Energy Medicine.* Tarcher/Putnam, 1998.
- Eden, Donna, and Feinstein, David. *The Energies of Love.* TarcherPerigee, 2014.

Energy, Chakras & Auras

- Judith, Anodea. *Wheels of Life: A User's Guide to the Chakra System.* Llewellyn Publications, 1987.
- Brennan, Barbara Ann. *Hands of Light: A Guide to Healing Through the Human Energy Field.* Bantam Books, 1988.
- Tiller, William. *Science and Human Transformation: Subtle Energies, Intentionality and Consciousness.* Pavior Publishing, 1997.
- Mulders, Evelyn. *The Essence of Sound: Full Spectrum Vibrational Healing for the Meridians, Chakras, Auric Fields & Figure Eight Energies* 2020

Dowsing & Divination

- Kruger, Hanna. *Pendulum Power: A Mystery You Can See, A Power You Can Feel.* Destiny Books, 1987.
- Martine, Cassandra Eason. *The Pendulum Kit.* Connections Book Publishing, 1999.
- Martineau, Greg. *Practical Dowsing: The Complete Guide to Finding What You Seek with a Pendulum.* Llewellyn Publications, 2012.
- Scherz, Erich. *The Divining Hand: The 500-Year-Old Mystery of Dowsing.* Harper & Row, 1989.

Inspiration & Blending Science with Mystery

- Tesla, Nikola. *Experiments with Alternate Currents of High Potential and High Frequency.* 1892.
- Dispenza, Joe. *Breaking the Habit of Being Yourself: How to Lose Your Mind and Create a New One.* Hay House, 2012.
- Sheldrake, Rupert. *The Sense of Being Stared At: And Other Aspects of the Extended Mind.* Crown Publishing, 2003.

Related Modalities

- Diamond, John. *Your Body Doesn't Lie.* Warner Books, 1979.
- Callahan, Roger. *Tapping the Healer Within.* McGraw-Hill, 2001. (Thought Field Therapy, related to muscle response testing.)
- Dawson Church. *The Genie in Your Genes: Epigenetic Medicine and the New Biology of Intention.* Elite Books, 2007.

Tip for Readers: This list is just the start. The best pendulum practice comes from experimenting yourself—then comparing your results with the wisdom of others.

Message From The Author

When I first picked up a pendulum, I had no idea where it would take me. I thought it was just a string with a weight on the end. But with every swing, I discovered something bigger—about energy, about intuition, and most importantly, about myself.

This book isn't here to tell you what to believe. It's here to invite you to experiment. To stay curious. To laugh when your pendulum gives you a "no" to pizza, and to wonder when it surprises you with clarity you didn't expect.

Whether you're a teenager just starting to explore your inner world, or an adult remembering the magic of asking questions, I hope these pages have shown you that the pendulum is more than a tool. It's a mirror. It reflects your hidden wisdom, your subconscious truth, and your ability to trust yourself.

My wish is that as you practice, you'll begin to notice something incredible: you don't need the pendulum forever. One day, you'll find yourself knowing the answer before you even ask. That's when you'll realize the pendulum has done its job—it trained you to trust your own inner compass.

So keep experimenting. Keep swinging. Keep listening. Because the journey doesn't end here—it's only just beginning.

With curiosity and gratitude,
Dr. Constance Santego

About the Author

If you've made it this far, you already know one of my secrets: I'm endlessly curious. Curious about energy, about why pendulums swing, and about how the tiniest shift in focus can open a whole new way of seeing yourself.

I didn't grow up thinking, *"One day, I'll write a book about pendulums."*
Honestly, the first time I picked one up, I thought it was just a neat little experiment. But the more I used it, the more I realized: this wasn't just about yes and no. It was about learning to trust my own inner compass.

That's why I wrote this book for you. Whether you're a teenager trying something new, or an adult who secretly still loves to play and explore, I wanted to create a guide that makes the pendulum fun, practical, and a little bit magical.

I've spent years studying and teaching energy healing, intuition, and the science of vibration—but at the end of the day, I'm just like you: still asking questions, still experimenting, still staying curious.

So if your pendulum has sparked something in you, I'm glad. Because this journey doesn't really end with me—it continues with you, every time you pick it up and ask, *"What happens if...?"*
Dr. Constance Santego, Ph.D., DNM

ALSO AVAILABLE

For additional information on

Constance Santego's

wide range of Motivational Products, Coaching Sessions,
Spiritual Retreats,
Live Events and Educational Programs

Go to

www.ConstanceSantego.ca

Follow on Instagram - Constance_Santego and
Facebook - constancesantegoo

Subscribe and receive Free Information and Meditations
on her
YouTube Channel - Constance Santego

Trade Paperback ISBN: 978-1-990062-49-0
eBook ISBN 978-1-990062-50-6

.